RESOURCES FOR
MIDDLE
CHILDHOOD

A SOURCE BOOK

Reference Books on
Family Issues

Vol. 12

**GARLAND REFERENCE LIBRARY
OF THE SOCIAL SCIENCES
(VOL. 433)**

REFERENCE BOOKS ON FAMILY ISSUES

RESOURCES FOR
MIDDLE
CHILDHOOD

A SOURCE BOOK

Deborah Lovitky Sheiman

Maureen Slonim

GARLAND PUBLISHING, INC.
NEW YORK & LONDON
1988

Library of Congress Cataloging-in-Publication Data
Sheiman, Deborah Lovitky.
    Resources for middle childhood / Deborah Lovitky Sheiman,
Maureen Slonim.
        p.   cm. — (Garland reference library of social science ; v.
433)
        Includes index.
        ISBN 0–8240–7777–6 (alk. paper)
        1. Child development. 2. Child development—Bibliography.
3. School children. 4. School children—Bibliography.   5.
Socialization. 6. Socialization—Bibliography. I. Slonim,
Maureen. II. Title. III. Series: Garland reference library of
social science ; v. 433.
HQ767.9.S48 1988
305.2'3—dc19   88-18046

Design by Renata Gomes

Printed on acid-free, 250-year-life paper
Manufactured in the United States of America

For our children
Laura and Jill Sheiman
Mark Slonim and Linda Slonim-Lauler

TABLE OF CONTENTS

FOREWORD

Middle childhood, also known as the elementary school years, is a stretch in the lifespan that Freud referred to as "latency"; the period lasting from the end of early childhood until the onset of puberty. Freud theorized that during this span the child has little interest in sex. Energy is spent on the process of becoming socialized.

Erik Erikson labeled this developmental space the stage of industry versus inferiority. A time when the child is a ready and eager learner. Society in general, and the educational system in particular, must provide appropriate learning opportunities and experiences for the child to master. Children limited in these experiences may become at risk for developing a life long feeling of inferiority.

Jean Piaget refers to these years as a time when the child's cognitive structure and logic improves. Parents and teachers view the middle childhood years as a time marked by major changes in the child's capacities and capabilities. Developmental growth pushes the child from a non-reader to a diligent learner, a ball roller to cartwheel contortionist, and a parent dependent being to one entrenched in the details of a social peer subculture.

The child in this stage focuses on skills needed in later life. It's a time filled with strict adherence to moral rules. Ethical concepts like fairness and loyalty become rigidly fixed.

Though the triumphs of the school years help establish a positive sense of self, it is not a period free from problems. School related difficulties become a source of trouble for many children. Making friends, adjusting to family stresses, and concentrating and understanding schoolwork can become horns of dilemma.

In the chapters that follow an attempt has been made to help the parent, teacher, and student of child development gain a better understanding of the growth and needs of the six to 12 year old child. Frequently asked questions about the impact of society on middle childhood, the meaning of children's play, how youngsters interact with their peers, and the role of the school and family in development are among the many issues discussed in the following pages. An annotated bibliography attached to each chapter allows the reader to delve further into a specific interest area of the middle years. *Resources for Middle Childhood* is designed to provide a handy reference to all who are concerned with this stage of child development.

Deborah Lovitky Sheiman, Ed.D.

Resources for
Middle Childhood

PHYSICAL DEVELOPMENT DURING MIDDLE CHILDHOOD

Physical development during the years from six to 12 appears less spectacular than that seen during the early childhood years. Boys and girls progress on a steady course marked by prepubescent growth spurts. Children grow about two to two-and-one-half inches and gain about five pounds per year. Girls are apt to be shorter and weigh less than boys at age six. By nine years this trend has been reversed, with girls surpassing boys in both height and weight. Even foot growth is rapid, necessitating frequent changes of shoe size until the age of 12.

Though height and weight are the most visible changes, the structure and function of the body gradually matures. Growth takes place in muscle, bone tissue, and the teeth. The reproductive organs and the sensory systems change. Development continues to follow cephalocaudal law, meaning growth proceeds from head to toe, from simple to complex, from gross to refined, and from large to small.

By the time six year olds have found their way into the elementary school, their heads have grown to ninety percent of adult size. Early and rapid brain development account for the large size of the head in comparison to the body. During the middle years only about a five percent increase in head size occurs. However, refinement of the brain and nervous system provides the background for the cognitive growth that takes place during these years.

Greater muscle strength, and ligaments not yet firmly attached to bones, make the school-age child as physically flexible as a contortionist. As muscles develop, children experience a stronger urge for physical activity. Nighttime growing pains result from developing muscles adapting and responding to the developing skeleton. Skeletal growth requires a greater supply of blood, ligaments that are not firmly attached, and space between the bones at the joints. Children's bones have proportionately more water and less minerals than adult bones. These factors render children more susceptible to muscle pulls and bone infections carried through the bloodstream.

Eyes, ears, and teeth undergo changes. Binocular vision is well developed by early middle childhood. Ear infections become less likely than in the early childhood years because of the lengthening, narrowing, and change of slant in the eustachian tubes. Hearing acuity is continuously increasing until around age 13.

Middle childhood marks the end of baby teeth. Around age six the first permanent tooth generally comes in. It is at this time that baby teeth begin to loosen. By age 12 all 20 baby teeth will be replaced with permanent teeth.   Girls usually lose their teeth earlier than boys.

Elementary school-age children often spend too little time on proper brushing and flossing of teeth and too much time ingesting candy and other cavity-producing food.   This results in the average child acquiring yearly cavities.   Parents should stress proper dental care and check-ups.   Use of a dentist-supplied fluoride treatment and plastic sealants brushed onto susceptible tooth surfaces help to reduce dental decay.   Toward the end of middle childhood many children require orthodontic appliances to correct irregularities of teeth and jaw.   Most children look forward to losing their baby teeth and enjoy wearing orthodontic braces.   These are signs of growing up.

Dramatic reproductive system changes during late middle childhood mark puberty.   Puberty is likely to take place between eight and 14 for girls and between 10 and 14 for boys.   In girls the first sign of puberty is breast buds, followed by pubic hair, and the first menstrual period occurring between ages 10 to 16.   Though the uterus has reached full maturity, reproductive ability is absent for about a year following the first period.

In boys the testes and the scrotum enlarge and pubic hair appears.   This is followed by penis growth and prostate gland and semenal vesicle enlargement.

Major growth spurts take place during puberty.   Girls gain in height and weight before menstruation.   An average of two and one half inches additional growth follows the menarche and brings girls to their approximate adult height.   In boys height spurts usually occur between the ages of 10 to 16.   About one year after this spurt boys may begin to experience irregular nocturnal emissions or "wet dreams."   This is normal and is the disengorgement of sperm produced by the testes.

Age of the onset of puberty has gradually declined during the twentieth century in the United States.   Early or late bloomers are likely to feel uncomfortable and different from their peers at an age when conformity is of utmost concern.   The age at which puberty occurs is controlled by heredity and environmental factors such as nutrition and health care.   Many pubescent children feel they don't look right.   They need encouragement and assurance that their bodies will eventually feel comfortable and look normal.   This is a time when parents must take and make the opportunities to discuss reproductive and sexual concerns with their children.   Children's books that deal with these topics can be used to start discussions.   Misinformation always has and will continue to be gotten on the streets. Parents should straightforwardly correct these myths and give their children honest answers.

Body image problems are complicated when children are overweight.   Children who are twenty percent heavier than they should be for their height are considered obese.   Overweight children see their bodies negatively.   Extra pounds limit their physical and athletic capacities. Heavy children are viewed as being more passive than active. Being overweight becomes a social obstacle. Insensitive and unthinking classmates give nicknames like "Fatso" and "Tub." Obese children may turn to food to find happiness because of their social rejection and exclusion. This can start an endless cycle of rejection and eating that leads to additional weight gain and possible maladjustment.

Heredity and environment are of concern in obesity. Children with two overweight parents are likely to also be overweight. If neither parent is overweight, chances are children in the family will not be obese. Overweight children are prone to elevated blood pressure and high serum cholesterol. Youngsters who spend their childhood years overweight are likely to also find themselves fighting the same weight problems throughout adulthood. It is a cause for debate among experts as to what the interaction of biological, heredity, environmental, and psychological factors are and their corresponding importance in producing an obese child. It is very difficult to determine the cause and effect relationship since researchers often find themselves asking the parallel question to what came first, the chicken or the egg? This has been exemplified in studies which have found that in obese children a rapid increase in cellularity occurred between the ages of five and seven while a similar increase did not occur in non-obese children until the ages of nine to 12. The question that arose from this was, is it obesity that caused the early cell increase or is the early increase just another manifestation of some unknown biological or physiological problem that caused obesity? It is known that children who become fat early in childhood have a greater number of adipose or fat cells than children who become obese later in life. Even if the child looses weight later in life, the number of adipose cells never decreases, the cells only shrink in size.

Obesity has multiple causes. Genetic inheritance, lack of physical exercise, plus a tendency to eat the wrong foods or overeat can contribute to children's weight problems. The best defense against childhood obesity is a caring parent. Parents should avoid using foods as bribes or rewards, or as punishments. Never encourage children to eat until their plates are clean. Allow them to eat until satisfied, not stuffed. Smaller portions can avoid wasted food. Allow children to leave the table when they are through eating. Bored children sitting at the table may take second portions or nibble on leftover food just to fill the time and thus overfill their stomachs.

Parents should avoid commenting or nagging children about their oversized bodies or poor eating habits. Instead, control the child's environment by only serving low calorie, healthy foods and leaving the high calorie cookies, candies, and snacks on the grocer's shelves. Select wholesome dietetic foods, low in fats and sugar, for children's snacks. Children should not feel that their parents' love and respect are based on their body size.

Parents can help their children select an active exercise program to help burn off calories. Obese children who are too embarrassed to be seen swimming or jogging in public might prefer activities they can do at home. Jumping rope or working out to an exercise tape are examples.

Too stringent weight control during middle childhood can also lead to problems. Children who don't eat enough can experience retarded growth and development. Too much pressure for absolute thinness during middle childhood can lead to anorexia (self-starvation) and bulimia (self-induced vomiting) during adolescence.

The healthy child who is shorter than his peers may also feel uncomfortable. There are many causes for short stature including chronic systemic disease, constitutional delay of growth, interuterine growth retardation including endocrine problems, and the most common cause, genetic tendency. Short parents have short children. Therefore, genetically a short child may grow at a normal rate for that child and have bone age appropriate for chronological age. Parents who question their child's lag in height and/or weight should consult a physician. Diagnosis of the causes of shortness focus attention on past growth, chronic illness, family growth patterns, and include physical examination and laboratory screening.

Lagging behind peers in height or weight can bruise self-image. The child's physical development sets limits not only on what the child can experience, but also to some extent on what he can learn. This stems from the child's need to be physiologically developed enough before he can handle certain tasks, such as sports skills. Thus, in a stage that Erik Erikson calls the time for industry and accomplishment,[1] the underdeveloped child may feel inferior and defeated. Parents and teachers guiding the child should provide opportunities for success and foster positive feelings about the child's abilities and accomplishments.

Vitamin supplements are generally not needed if a proper diet is being consumed. However, parents with children on calorie-reduced diets may feel more comfortable giving a dietary supplement to ensure proper nutrition and avoid marginal vitamin deficiency. One should choose a balanced multi-vitamin, multi-mineral supplement that provides 100% of U.S. RDA. Parents should be sure that there is an expiration date on the package since vitamins lose their potency over time and should avoid vitamins that contain sugar or artificial sweeteners. These mean more empty calories and added chemicals, besides establishing the dangerous belief that pills can taste like candy. Parents should not give children excess doses of vitamins. Nutrients interact with each other. Vitamins consumed over the body's actual needs are either excreted or stored. Serious imbalances can evolve if there are excesses. Consumption of large doses of vitamins can raise

---

[1]Erik Erikson, *Childhood and Society*. (New York: Norton, 1963).

a child's body maintenance level, and in rare cases cause toxicity. The elementary school years are generally a healthy period. Communicable diseases are less common than in early childhood. Minor respiratory and gastro-intestinal illnesses can account for an occasional school absence. Allergies ranging from food sensitivity, such as lactose intolerance, to hay fever, are common recurring problems. Parents may find that such allergies may necessitate a change in routine. For example, lactose sensitive children may need to request orange juice rather than milk with their school lunch or require pills to aid in the digestion of dairy products. Children whose allergies affect their ears and hearing ability may need to change their seats to the front of the classroom.

Severe health problems during middle childhood can tax a child's ability to cope. An estimated 10 percent of American children suffer physical disorders lasting three months or longer.[2] Each child's unique makeup of genetic endowment, constitutional traits, developmental capabilities, and past experiences contribute to the adaptive capacity to cope.

Parents and medical practitioners alike should remember that children have increased psychological as well as physical needs when faced with illness. Fear of falling behind in school work, as well as seclusion from peers, worries children. Imagined and exaggerated stories and myths about shots and medical procedures may influence the amount of discomfort children perceive. Children need to be reminded that pain connected with an illness will subside over time. Children know that shots and medical procedures can hurt. Parents should never tell them otherwise. Instead, they should remind them that a shot hurts just for a short time and then it is over. Children appreciate truth and straightforward answers.

When illness requires hospitalization, as it does for millions of children each year, parents should prepare their child as much as possible. With a parent present, the doctor should inform the child of the need for hospitalization. Children do not ask many questions at this time. The elementary school years are a period when children require time to think about and clarify their own fears. They need to talk to their peers and/or siblings, and then ask the adults in authority their questions. Parents and doctors alike should make known the reasons for the hospitalization, the procedures involved, and what the consequences of these procedures will be. In other words, what will be relieved or prevented by the hospitalization. Doctors should be honest in their estimate of the length of stay and the course of hospitalization.

Middle childhood is a time of fears of hospitalizations. The greatest fear is that of separation. While children in the very early

---

[2]Audrey McCollum, *The Chronically Ill Child*. (New Haven: Yale University Press, 1981) p.v.

elementary years may view separation as permanent, older elementary school-age children may perceive it as a form of rejection. Parents should remain with their children as much as they are able and hospital regulations permit. This contributes to the feeling of security and adjustment to hospital routine. Hospitalized children need to be reminded that though life is continuing on at home, they are missed and things are not the same in their absence. They need to be reminded that they will be coming home.

Surgery brings additional problems. Children fear change or disfigurement associated with surgery. They need assurance that what is happening is for the best and after any surgery they will still be the same person. Parents should avoid associating anesthesia with going to sleep. By middle childhood children have known of pets that were put to sleep. Children may fear never waking up from the surgery. Instead, the child should be told that anesthetics make him or her unaware and not able to feel what is happening. When the anesthesia is taken away, the sensation is similar to waking up, but that the child may feel discomfort and be in a recovery room and not able to see their parents immediately. Children fear the loss of self-control and self-awareness while under anesthesia.

It is normal for both children and parents to be nervous when facing illness and hospitalization. Regressive tendencies, outbursts of emotion and general anxiety can occur or persist during or after a hospital stay. Supportive family members can help the child cope until all is back to normal. This is a time for communicating and parents' clarifying the misconceptions that children hold concerning illness and health care.

Enuresis, or bedwetting in children who don't evidence physical disorders, may persist as a problem in some children during the middle years. This condition is more evident in boys than girls. Parents should seek the advice of a pediatrician to eliminate or control this potentially psychologically traumatic problem. A drug such as Imipramine which permits greater than usual bladder expansion and reduces the need to void in the middle of the night can allow an enuretic child to sleep over a friend's house accident free. This approach must be used under a physician's direction, since any prescription drug intervention can produce side effects and must be used cautiously.

Another approach to curing the bed-wetting problem is a urine alarm system. This is an electronic device, attached to underpants or a mattress pad, that sounds a buzzer when wetness from urination occurs. The urine alarm system which has been around in earlier forms since the 1930s is safe and easy to use and can be purchased in pharmacies or through healthcare catalogs (Sears).

Neither of these treatment methods (urine alarm or medication) have a 100 percent success rate. However, both are quite popular and an individual child's expected success is best determined by analyzing the characteristics of the child's problem. In any treatment approach there is always a percentage of cases expected to not respond and to require retreatment.

Sleep and bedtime problems may persist throughout middle childhood. Most sleep-related problems are transient. However, any severe or long-term problem should be shared with a pediatrician. The most common sleep-related problems are parasomnias, such as sleepwalking, nightmares, and sleep bruxism. Sleep/wake schedule disorders can also trouble children, particularly in the later years.

Sleepwalking is thought to have genetic and maturational components since often there is a family history. Most children who sleepwalk eventually outgrow it. Children recall little of what they say or do during these episodes. Since sleepwalking children are not coherent during these episodes, parents should be careful to protect them from dangers. Gates should be put over staircase entrances and parents should take away objects that could potentially be harmful to the sleepwalking child.

Sleep bruxism refers to teeth grinding or clenching produced as the jaw muscles contract rhythmically. Anxiety is frequently causative. Children whose parents have bruxism are more likely to have this condition. For most children this problem alleviates itself. However, if this persists over a long period the family dentist can construct a tooth protecting prosthesis. The use of biofeedback techniques have also been successful in reducing the incidence of sleep bruxism in severe cases.

Most children suffer from occasional nightmares. Since they occur during REM sleep, dream content can usually be remembered. Nightmares in and of themselves suggest no pathology. However, they do disturb the child's sleep and create anxiety over going to bed. Children can be comforted by recalling and talking over the bad dream with their parents. Reassuring and comforting parents can help the scared child relax and go back to sleep. If nightmares occur very frequently, the parents should consult their pediatrician. The child may be dealing with some upsetting experience that he or she cannot cope with or verbalize.

A common sleep schedule disorder of middle childhood is Delayed Sleep Phase Syndrome. Symptoms include fatigue during the day, the inability to fall asleep at night, and the inability to get up in the morning. The actual number of hours of sleep is generally normal. Over a period of time the child goes to bed later and thus gets up later and later. The rhythms of the body have changed. A strict bedtime and getting-up time will keep children on schedule and should alleviate Delayed Sleep Phase Syndrome.

Though middle childhood is a period of refining physical skills and the desire to acquire new skills runs high, stress on fitness is still necessary. Children spend a large part of their day behind desks in the classroom and additional hours passively watching television. Physical activity helps to rejuvenate the body and the mind. Muscles must be used on a regular basis at a level higher than the normal activity level in order to attain physical fitness. Developing skills in swimming, tennis, biking and gymnastics give the body a workout. Parents should consider whether they want their sons and daughters to engage in contact sports or team sports. Before skilled sports playing can be achieved children must have the necessary muscular development. Maturation precedes learning. Learning becomes skill with practice and motivation. Coaches of children's team sports should never push children more than their physical development allows. Not only will the child not learn to play well, but actual damage to the body can occur.

Damaged self-image also results from not performing as well as coaches might like. Children need to play games to develop the skills necessary for social inclusion. To know how to play means to be chosen. To play only to win stresses competition at all costs and takes away the fun and social lessons to be learned from the game. Not all children enjoy team play and not all children are well coordinated. During the middle childhood years major changes in perceptual motor abilities occur that do promote coordination. Visual dominance takes over as a way of regulating motor behavior. Reliance on multi-sensory systems with increased discriminatory and differential abilities helps the middle school-aged child become more physically precise, quick, and coordinated.

It is important that parents gain insight into how a child's body grows and works, as well as some of the common factors that can influence health and welfare. Children frequently are apprehensive of the changes their developing body brings. Communicative, sympathetic parents can help their children cope and understand that physically growing up may not be quite as bad as their worrying and imagination suggests.

Parents should also be warned that age ranges indicated in this discussion are norms and averages. Children can fall to either the high or low end of the spectrum and still be "normal." Being an exception from a growth norm does not necessarily make a child abnormal. If parents are concerned that their child falls short of the growth norms or exceed these, they should consult their physician. Each child is an individual.

Healthiness is a goal the whole family can work toward. Children can be taught to accept responsibility for developing and maintaining habits that promote good health and nutrition and a strong body. Any distress, dysfunction, or disability in a child should not go unnoticed. Most likely the problem is minor. However, any problem for a child warrants a parent's concern and empathy. Tender loving care can frequently be the best medicine. Honest answers to children's questions about their bodies and illness can promote a realistic concept of health and help elementary school-aged children to be good caretakers of their bodies.

BIBLIOGRAPHY

Akins, Dianna. *The Hospitalized Child*. New York: Plenum, 1981.

A comprehensive volume of abstracts and bibliography focusing on the behavioral and developmental consequences of short-term, long-term, and recurrent hospitalization during childhood. Over 500 citations are listed. The bibliography is a helpful guide to the literature in this area.

Anderson, Peggy. *Children's Hospital*. New York: Bantam, 1986.

Anderson discusses severely afflicted boys and girls, their parents, and health care professionals who serve them. The author, a member of the staff of Children's Hospital of Philadelphia, reports on the actual happenings of this large, excellent, pediatric institution. Case studies are included.

Balter, Lawrence. *Dr. Balter's Child Sense*. New York: Poseidon Press, 1986.

Offers practical advice on handling common concerns, such as sleep problems, during childhood. Helps parents understand why a child behaves in a certain way and offers practical, jargon-free advice. This book focuses on the younger child.

Behrstock, Barry. *The Parent's When-Not-to-Worry Book*. New York: Harper & Row, 1981.

Demythologizes many time-honored misconceptions about everyday child health care. Practical advice, based on recent medical findings and proven pediatric practices, is given.

Bindler, Ruth. *The Parent's Guide to Pediatric Drugs*. New York: Harper & Row, 1985.

Explains why each drug is used, how it is administered, time needed for the drug to work, unintended side effects, possible drug and food interactions, contra-indications to use of a drug, and proper storage. General brand and generic name indexes are given. An essential home reference.

Boston Children's Medical Center. *Child Health Encyclopedia*. New York: Dell, 1986.

Advice from more than 80 medical experts is given in this volume, making it a complete guide to the health and diseases affecting children. A welcome addition to any household with children.

Brace, Edward. *The Pediatric Guide to Drugs and Vitamins*. New York, HP Books, 1987.

This revised paperback edition describes the most commonly prescribed drugs for children. Valuable information on drug dosage and possible side effects is given. A helpful home health reference.

Brace, Edward, and John Pacanowski. *Childhood Symptoms*. New York: Harper & Row, 1985.

Includes over 500 cross-referenced, alphabetically arranged entries on a wide range of childhood medical problems. Each entry provides the specific condition or symptom, its probable significance, and recommended handling. Also given is a list of questions parents should ask themselves before phoning the physician.

Brody, Jane. *Jane Brody's Nutrition Book*. New York: Norton & Co., 1981.

Mrs. Brody is the personal health columnist for the New York Times. Her book covers, in detail, most issues concerning food and nutrition for every age group. This comprehensive volume is an effective reference.

Brooks-Gunn, Jeanne. *Girls at Puberty*. New York: Plenum, 1983.

Experts from the field of anthropology, psychology, sociology, and medicine discuss puberty. Topics covered include nutrition, menarche, early sexuality, and the cognitive effects of puberty. Broad coverage is given.

Calderone, Mary S., and James W. Ramey. *Talking with Your Child about Sex, Questions and Answers for Children from Birth to Puberty*. New York: Random, 1984.

Employs a useful question and answer format. It is a helpful guide in understanding what children really want to know about sex, and when and how to tell them.

Coffin, Lewis. *Children's Nutrition*. Santa Barbara, Calif.: Capra Press, 1984.

Deals with the nutrition of children from birth through puberty. Touches upon specifics in nutrition such as the relationship of fluoride, minerals, and sugar to the health of a child. A good book for parents.

Coulter, Harris, and Barbara Fisher. *DPT: A Shot in the Dark*. New York: Warner, 1986.

Explores the current controversy surrounding this vaccination given to 96% of all American children. They discuss the development of the vaccine and its side effects. The questionable safety of the DPT shot is examined. Parents will find this book interesting.

Diagram Group. *Child's Body*. New York: Bantam, 1979.

Contains numerous charts and diagrams and is designed to provide clear explanations of every aspect of the body's functioning, care, and development. Chapters include discussion of anatomy and physiology, child development, illness and disease, food and exercise, and first aid. The information is comprehensive and statistics are offered in interesting ways. Material in this book was presented to a team of practicing pediatricians and child-care experts for their advice and review. The detailed table of contents and good index help make the book easy to use.

Ferber, Richard. *Solve Your Child's Sleep Problem*. New York: Fireside, 1986.

A helpful guide for parents with children who have sleep problems. The basics of good sleep habits are outlined and the causes of sleep problems such as bed wetting, sleep phase shifts, and snoring are explored. The author is the director of the Sleep Clinic at Children's Hospital in Boston.

Gittelman, Rachel. *Anxiety Disorders of Childhood*. New York: Guilford Press, 1986.

A comprehensive review of childhood anxiety disorders. This volume follows a developmental sequence in its analysis of anxieties. It provides a valuable resource for clinicians and educators.

Goldsmith, Robert. *Nutrition and Learning*. Bloomington, Ind.: Phi Delta Kappa, 1980.

The relationship of nutrition to cognitive and motor development is examined in this small volume from the respected Phi Delta Kappa Educational Foundation. Specific nutritionally related learning problems are discussed. Positive preventive nutrition education is considered from the viewpoint of the schools.

Goodwin, Mary T., and Gerry Pollen. *Creative Food Experiences for Children*. Washington, D.C.: Center for Science in the Public Interest, 1980.

Helps parents, teachers, and nutritionists involve children in the preparation of whole foods and other food-related experiences. Its thoughtful organization enables the user to connect these experiences with other educational goals, such as language skills, mathematical skills, arts and crafts, and social awareness.

Griffith, H.W. *Pediatrics for Parents: A Guide to Child Health.* New York: Plume, 1983.

A child health care encyclopedia. Provides a quick reference guide for parents. This volume covers the years from infancy through adolescence.

Hollingsworth, C.E. *Coping with Pediatric Illness.* New York: SP Books, 1983.

Looks at the psychological effects of specific illnesses and disabilities and provides recommendations for coping with these problems. The impact of pediatric illness on the parent and child is discussed. For professionals in child health.

Jampolsky, Jerry. *Another Look at the Rainbow--Straight from the Siblings.* Tiburon, Calif.: Celestial Arts, 1984.

The text and drawing in this well-presented book deal with children's attitudes and concerns about having a sibling with a life threatening illness. Highly recommended for parents, children, teachers, and health care professionals.

Jampolsky, Jerry. *There Is a Rainbow behind Every Dark Cloud.* Tiburon, Ca.: Celestial Arts, 1981.

Looks at the attitudes and thoughts of terminally ill children toward sickness and dying. Excellently and professionally presented. Children's drawings are included. Recommended for anyone who is involved with children faced with life threatening illness.

Jones, Monica. *Home Care for the Chronically Ill or Disabled Child.* New York: Harper & Row, 1985.

Provides help for families with chronically ill or disabled children. Chapters discuss meeting the child's medical needs, daily physical needs, social needs and education, as well as meeting the needs of the entire family.

Kersey, Katharine. *Helping Your Child Handle Stress: The Parents' Guide to Recognizing and Solving Childhood Problems.* New York: Acropolis, 1985.

Suggests strategies for coping with stress. Pointers are given on how to listen to children, how to clear up misconceptions, and how to hear clues in children's talk and play.

Kirschenbaum, Daniel. *Treating Childhood and Adolescent Obesity.* Elmsford, N.Y.: Pergamon Books, 1987.

Presents approaches to combat child obesity. Elements of success in treating childhood weight problems are discussed. The focus of this volume is on behavioral principles which can be applied to control eating and increase exercising. A technical work best appreciated by health care professionals.

Krasnegor, Norman. *Child Health Behavior*. New York: Wiley, 1986.

Covers information on clinical issues and major research areas. Reviews include topic areas such as obesity, primary care and developmental determinants of behavior. For health care professionals.

LeBow, Michael. *Child Obesity*. New York: Springer, 1983.

A comprehensive discussion of childhood obesity is covered in this volume. Research, treatment regimens, and epidemiology of the problem are reviewed. Practitioners, researchers, and students of the problem will find this book useful.

Lynch, Annette. *Redisigning School Health Services*. New York: Human Sciences Press, 1983.

Argues that school health services fail to meet the needs of today's children. Cites the absence of an epidemiologic approach and inefficient use of staff and resources. Presented as a model system that expands the role of the school nurse, this book is of interest to individuals concerned with delivering a more complete health care system to school-age children.

McCollum, Audry. *The Chronically Ill Child*. New Haven: Yale University Press, 1981.

A well-written, sensitive guide for parents and professionals who are working with children with chronic health problems. The author helps to refocus and clarify the many theoretical and practical issues faced by professionals and families dealing with the chronically ill child.

McGrath, Patrick. *Pediatric and Adolescent Behavioral Medicine*. New York: Springer, 1983.

Reviews the assessment, management, and treatment of selected medical problems common to children. Thorough and well-written. It can be a valuable resource to any professional child health practitioner.

McKnew, Donald, Leon Cytryn, and Herbert Hahraas. *Why Isn't Johnny Crying?* New York: Norton, 1985.

Feelings of sadness and depression are generally associated with adults under stress. The authors bring to light this same phenomenon as experienced by children. Problems associated with depression have been identified as well as approaches to help it. Informative reading for anyone living or working with children.

McWilliams, Margaret. *Nutrition for the Growing Years*, 3rd ed. New York: Wiley, 1980.

McWilliams considers nutrition from a theoretical yet practical standpoint. A chapter is devoted to sound scientific discussion of the interrelationship of nutrition to cognitive development. The role of childhood diet in preventative and maintenance health care is examined. Attention is given to the effects of adequate and inadequate nutrition on the developmental stages of infancy and childhood.

Madaras, Lynda. *What's Happening to My Body? A Growing-Up Guide for Mothers and Daughters*. New York: Newmarket, 1983.

Helps the young girl understand the changes taking place in her body during puberty. Increases self-acceptance and fosters mother-daughter discussion of this subject.

Madaras, Lynda. *The "What's Happening to My Body" Book for Boys, A Growing-Up Guide for Parents and Sons*. New York: Newmarket, 1984.

Discusses the changes in a boy's body during puberty. It is a helpful guide that a parent and son can read together and the child can keep for easy reference and support. Fosters a sense of communication between parent and child.

Martin, Richard. *A Parent's Guide to Childhood Symptoms*. New York: St. Martin's, 1983.

Logical approach that alerts parents to the first signs and symptoms of illness. Fifteen chapters outline a variety of ailments. A handy home reference.

Nash, Eric, and Leif Terdal. *Behavioral Assessment of Childhood Disorders*. New York: Guilford, 1981.

Blends methods, theory and observation with suggestions for remediation. Looks closely at the areas of obesity, enuresis and encopresis, and sleep disturbances. Social skill deficits are discussed in depth. For professionals.

National Cancer Institute. *A Resource for Parents of Children with Cancer*. Bethesda, Md.: Office of Cancer Communications, 1979.

This outstanding book is available free to the public. It provides basic nutrition information for cancer patients, practical suggestions for avoiding and handling feeding problems, and seven different special diets. A large wall chart is included. This resource is largely the result of parental contributions and involvement.

National Research Council. *Recommended Dietary Allowances*. Washington, D.C.: National Academy of Sciences, 1985.

A guide to the proper nutrients necessary to sustain healthy life. It has been revised every five years since 1943. A reference for parents and professionals.

Pantell, Robert H., James Fries, and Donald Vickery. *Taking Care of Your Child: A Parent's Guide to Medical Care*. Reading, Mass.: Addison-Wesley, 1984.

Presents detailed, step-by-step instructions pertaining to all aspects of home care for children. There are helpful "decision-making charts" that parents can use in deciding when to call the doctor or when the problem can be handled with home care. Another unique feature is the "Home Pharmacy" chapter that discusses a number of medicines for treating common symptoms.

Peavy, Linda S., and Andrea L. Pagenkopf. *Grow Healthy Kids!* New York: Grosset and Dunlop, 1980.

A documented guide to nutrition for children. Offers medically sanctioned guidelines that can make the concept of sound nutrition habits a reasonable, attainable goal. Contains practical, easy-to-use meal pattern guides for the preparation of well-balanced menus designed for child appeal.

Pfeffer, Cynthia. *The Suicidal Child*. New York: Guilford, 1986.

Suicide is one of the top 10 causes of death among six to 12 year olds. This startling rise in the number of completed and/or attempted suicides of pre-adolescents is examined in this book. Focus is given to risk factors, characteristics, causes, assessment, and treatments. Special attention is given to the involvement of family and school.

Pipes, Peggy. *Nutrition in Infancy and Childhood*. London: C.V. Mosby, 1981.

Stresses the importance of proper food intake in order to facilitate normal growth, development, and overall functioning. It is especially helpful in identifying possible vitamin or nutrient-specific deficiencies and the resulting problems. It also tells how diets can be tailored to different children, whether children are over or underactive, or suffering from specific allergies.

Rutter, Michael, Carroll Izard, and Peter Read. *Depression in Young People.* New York: Guilford, 1986.

Researchers in clinical and developmental areas have long been aware that childhood can be a troubled time. It is the goal of this volume to bring together the contributions from fields studying depression in young people. This book is an up-to-date review of childhood depression in social, cognitive, and biological terms.

Schaefer, Charles. *Childhood Encopresis and Enuresis: Causes and Therapy.* New York: Van Nostrand Reinhold, 1979.

Book discusses the causes of encopresis and enuresis dysfunctions of the bowel and bladder. Suggestions on how to handle these problems, as well as effective procedures for treatment are indicated. This book has wide appeal to parents, child care, and health care workers alike.

Silberstein, Warren P., and Lawrence Galton. *Helping Your Child Grow Slim.* New York: Simon and Schuster, 1982.

Many personal examples are given of the overweight child in this book. Dr. Silberstein was an overweight child. The focus is on the prevention of childhood obesity. This book does not deal with obesity as an individual problem to be overcome but rather a syndrome requiring family efforts.

Smith, Lendon H. *Foods for Healthy Kids.* New York: McGraw-Hill, 1981.

Advises parents on the prevention, treatment, and cure of physical and behavioral problems that have relevance to diet, sleep disturbances, allergies, mood swings, and hyperactivity. Resource lists are included for free and inexpensive information and materials. There is a useful bibliography attached.

Stoppard, Miriam. *Baby & Child A to Z Medical Handbook.* New York: HP Books, 1986.

A commonsense approach to children's medical problems. The book contains detailed illustrations and a chart of the child's body that helps to explain diagnoses. The author is a British health educator who has written 11 books and hosts a medical television program in England.

Stuart, Howard. *The Healthy Child.* Cambridge, Mass.: Harvard University Press, 1979.

Covers the physical, psychological, and social development of the child through adolescence. It explains how children's perception of their bodies can affect both how they see themselves and also how others see them. Also included is a discussion on children's biological patterns as well specific racial and familial inheritance that determines physical attributes.

Tseng, R. *The Relationship between Nutrition and Student Achievement, Behavior and Health. A Review of the Literature*. Tacoma, Wash.: Biosocial Publications, 1980.

Reviews, analyzes, and comments on the literature of achievement, behavior, and health. Discussion of topics include listlessness, apathy, and lack of activity. Technical but clear.

Walker, C.E., and M.C. Roberts, eds. *Handbook of Clinical Child Psychology*. New York: Wiley, 1983.

Provides informative thought on topics such as children's hospitalization and medical care, and health services in the elementary school. Each area of coverage is followed by an extensive bibliography. Technical and written for the professional.

Weiss, Gabrielle, and Lily Hechtman. *Hyperactive Children Grown Up*. New York: Guilford, 1986.

Begins with an overview then proceeds to provide a developmental analysis of hyperactivity. Symptoms are described. Treatment is discussed. Careful attention is paid to the hyperactive child in the elementary school. Useful to clinicians, students, teachers, and parents.

Weiner, Jerry. *Diagnosis and Psychopharmocology of Childhood and Adolescent Disorders*. New York: Wiley, 1985.

Provides valuable coverage of the use of psychoactive medication in childhood disorders. Theoretical and diagnostic considerations are given. The presentation is organized according to the diagnostic categories of DSM III. Helpful to the clinician.

Winick, Myron. *Growing Up Healthy*. New York: William Morrow, 1982.

Explains the latest scientific thinking about childhood nutrition from conception to adolescence. Discusses iron deficiency, lactose intolerance, obesity in the young child, snacking, hyperactivity diets, role of nutrition in caring for the sick child, training diets for young athletes, and excessive dieting and anorexia in adolescence. The author is one of the nation's leading experts in childhood nutrition and health.

Winick, Myron. *Society's Child: Nutrition in Children, Diet and Disorders*. Nutley, N.J.: LaRoche Laboratories, 1980.

Views nutrition from a sensible, well-balanced diet approach. The author dispels the many myths of megavitamin therapy and points out the potential dangers. Arguments pertaining to possible hazards of salt, sugar, fat, and food additives are critically examined. This publication is recommended for its scientific treatment of current issues.

Wolman, Benjamin. *Psychological Aspects of Obesity: A Handbook*. New York: Van Nostrand Reinhold, 1981.

Distinguished experts in the field of obesity trace the psychological roots of this problem. Etiology, symptomatology, and treatment methods are discussed. Suggested for health care professionals.

Wunderlich, Ray Jr., and Dwight Kalita. *Nourishing Your Child*. New Canaan, Conn.: Keats Publishing, 1984.

Written for parents who wish to nourish their child for protection against disease and illness. Deals with handling many of the common problems of childhood through proper nutrition and diet.

PSYCHOSOCIAL DEVELOPMENT DURING MIDDLE CHILDHOOD

Psychiatrists and child development specialists use the term "latency" in referring to the period of middle childhood. The term latency was first introduced in 1905 by Sigmund Freud in describing that period of childhood that begins with resolution of the Oedipus Complex and ends with the first manifestations of puberty. Freud used the term strictly in relation to psychosocial development, describing these as years in which sexual drives became quiescent, or latent.

Over the years, different theorists have disputed Freud's characterization, and the term latency, if used at all, has been modified to denote a "period" or "state" of latency. A modern characterization of this period embodies not only sexual development, but also social, emotional, moral, and intellectual development.

Basically, the middle age of childhood is a non-stressful period of relative stability, a period of important changes in cognitive abilities and psychological characteristics. This is the school-age period, when school-related experiences become increasingly influential. This is a quiet time psychologically, allowing a child to direct all his energies to learning, and to strengthen his identity and self-concepts. It is a period when the child consolidates his image of himself in relation to the world. Parents and teachers alike will often describe children this age as "delightful." It is almost a calm before the storm of adolescent rebellion.

Typical latency-age children are generally well-behaved, and eager to please adults, even those not present. They are proud of their parents and emulate their behavior. They have a strong sense of right and wrong, and rules are of major importance. They participate with enthusiasm and seriousness in group activities such as scouts and sports. Their energy level seems boundless. They are avid collectors of items such as coins, stamps, and trading cards, and are often "specialists" in what they collect.

Friendships are generally with the same sex, intense, and among boys, apt to be long-lasting. Girls, on the other hand, tend to change "best friends" frequently. Clubs with secret symbols, rituals, and select memberships have a special appeal. Boys and girls may be friends with one another, but such friendships are often the subject of much teasing.

Latency-age children love humor, especially puns, jokes, and riddles. As their attention and interest span widens, they welcome family vacations and trips to museums. They have an active sexual curiosity, masturbation is common; this is the era of "playing doctor

and nurse."
   Psychosocial development is usually studied in the context of
child development, psychology, human behavior, and allied professions.
Of these, the work of Erikson and Piaget is most relevant to psychosocial development during latency. Different theorists may use different terminology and different methodology, but in general, their
work is compatible and mutually reinforcing.
   Erikson's concepts of development, though grounded in the psychosexual theory of Freud, emphasizes the psychosocial development
of man. To Erikson, personality development occurs in a sequence of
"The Eight Stages of Man," each with a conflict to be resolved.
The middle years of childhood comprise the fourth stage. The
stage-specific task is to develop a sense of industry, or competence.
Failure to do so results in a sense of inferiority. To Erikson, industry means being busy and learning to complete something. These
are the years in which children learn to use and master the tools and
toys of their particular culture. If children fail to develop the basic
motor, social, and intellectual skills for success, they develop a sense
of inadequacy. Children this age need to feel a sense of accomplishment among their peers and their families.
   Piaget was a Swiss psychologist with an avid interest in epistemology, a branch of philosophy concerned with how knowledge is
acquired. Piaget observed children in minute detail, how they be-
haved, how they solved problems, and what specifically they said and
did. In Piagetian theory, there are four sequential periods of cognitive development, and it is essential to master one stage before ad-
vancing to the next higher level. Maturation, physical experience,
and social and environmental interaction are essential for cognitive
development and progress.
   Piaget's third period, ages 7 to 11, is The Period of Concrete
Logical Operations, a time of "hands-on-learning." These are the
years in which children master the concepts related to causality: conservation, seriation, classification, time, distance and speed. These
concepts of Piaget are defined in the chapter on Cognitive Development. With these concepts of Erikson and Piaget as a foundation, it
is possible to explore psychosocial development in more meaningful
detail.
   School entrance requires the resolution of several tasks--the
ability to separate from the mother, the ability to contact and interact with a new adult, and the ability to develop a meaningful relationship with peers. Subsequently, the major developmental tasks to
master are: academic skills; a high level of motivation for learning; a
crystallization of sex-role identity; the development of moral standards and conscience; learning how to deal appropriately with conflict
and anxiety. The ability to develop meaningful peer relationships remains significant.
   This is the time of becoming social. In doing so, the child must
cease to think of his parents as omnipotent. As he becomes exposed

to varying types of authority and expectations, he compares his parents and ultimately sees them in a more human role. In Piagetian theory, these are the complimentary processes of assimilation and accommodation, a means of seeking equilibrium, or harmony, between the world and the individual's view of the world. To Piaget, this constant seeking of equilibrium is the primary motivation for cognitive development.

In becoming socialized, children this age must learn to concentrate when working alone (reflexion), and to collaborate effectively in groups. Reflexion involves the evolution of logical thought processes (mental operations) and the ability to think about concrete existing objects and people. Logical thought process involves a cause and effect relation, as opposed to earlier intuitive-level thinking. Effective group collaboration depends on the ability to avoid confusing one's own goals and ideas with those of others. By age eight, the child is aware of himself as an individual, and is interested in evaluating his own performance and relationship with others.

One of the major tasks of middle childhood is learning how to belong. Children learn to identify with peers of their own sex. This is part of the process of developing a sexual and a cultural identity. Having a "best friend" is helpful in developing a sense of identity, a sense of belonging, and a sense of affirmation of values. Social development requires that children learn the correct use of language in order to exchange ideas with others. Language is important not only for group relationships, but also for learning.

This is also the period in which children develop the social skills of learning rules and morality. Children of seven or eight consider rules that are laid down by adults to be sacred and unchangeable. They think rigidly in terms of what is right and what is wrong. This changes completely by about the age of ten, when children no longer accept rules laid down unilaterally by adults. They still respect rules with fervor, but they expect to participate in establishing the rules. This is most clearly demonstrated by their group games. Now the children playing the games make the rules, which can be changed only if everyone so agrees.

Their sense of morality also changes with maturation. Children under the age of ten feel that punishment for a misdeed should be determined by the amount of damage done. They can accept blame if they feel that they are being treated with fairness. Being fair becomes a consideration of major importance. By age ten, a strong sense of justice is apparent. The ten-year-old is more apt to be concerned about what is wrong than with what is right. Responsibility for misdeeds is determined by whether the act was deliberate or accidental. Children are generally more harsh than adults in their moral judgement. Mutual respect and cooperation is essential for moral development. Initially this develops between children, but eventually extends between child and adult. A true sense of morality develops slowly. It is not based on fear of punishment, but rather of concern for others.

An important milestone in social understanding is the ability to sense the thoughts, intentions, and feelings of others. Subsequent to children's ability to empathize is the realization that they and their thoughts can also be perceived and understood by others. This milestone is usually achieved by age ten.

Children develop their sense of self-worth in several interrelated ways. They are conscious of how others treat them and respond to them. Parental love and support, together with discipline and structure in their home life, enable a child to develop a positive self-image. Children of latency-age are characteristically concerned with body image, or how they perceive that others view them. A child's self-image develops in correlation to body image and is basic to all ego functioning.

Children need recognition for their accomplishments in school, at home, and in extra-curricular activities. They are afraid of failure, of being labeled a loser. This fear of failure is a driving force to improve, to try harder, to succeed. During latency, children begin to think about their future, about a career, about marriage. The parameters of these future musings will generally reflect their socioeconomic status, their culture, and their heritage.

Emotional development is closely intertwined with psychological and biological development in middle childhood. At the same time that physical growth is becoming more gradual, the central nervous system is becoming "fine-tuned," the child is developing a self-identity apart from his parents, and a sense of morality is unfolding. It is no wonder, therefore, that children this age exhibit a wide range of emotions. A child's emotions will reflect how he feels about his physical status, his ability to get along with his peers, his ability to master his schoolwork, and the emotional climate of his home and family, along with his own innate temperament.

This is an age of contradiction, especially where emotions are concerned. Children may convey an "I don't care" attitude when, in reality, they are very sensitive to criticism. The desire to please and the need for approval are paramount in latency. Some children may demonstrate boldness, others shyness. They desire increasing independence from home and family, yet harbor worries of being alone and a fear of the dark and the unknown. They can be obsessed with neatly organizing a collection of rocks, while their room and clothing are in total disarray. They resist parental control over how they look and what they do, yet seek and need parental approval. They can be moved to tears by injustice to strangers, yet be cruel and tactless to friends. They can be exasperating to live with at home, yet be the perfect model of decorum away from home. Overall, fortunately, cheerful emotions far outweigh the unpleasant episodes. Negative behavior is usually superficial and short-lived. During these middle years of childhood, personality characteristics begin to crystallize.

The fears and fantasies that children experience in middle childhood are generally age-related, and as such, another indicator of how well the child is mastering the tasks of latency. Children six to eight are apt to be fearful of monsters or ghosts or dragons or "the boogeyman." This usually indicates that they still believe in animism, attributing life-like characteristics to inanimate objects. They may be afraid of the dark, or of being left alone. Often, such fears are precipitated by a frightening movie, story, or television program. They might also indicate that the child is vulnerable to being teased by older children.

By age eight, there may still be a lingering fear of the dark. Otherwise, fears begin to be more reality-based, such as fear of snakes, of fighting, and (the characteristic fear of latency) of criticism or failure. Most children, especially when there is a crisis or family conflict, fear parental loss or abandonment. At about this age, children are more apt to become worriers than to have outright fears. Elementary school children will fear, or worry about, dangers and possible accidents consistent with their environment. Dreams, if they do occur, are usually pleasant and about everyday occurrences. As with younger children, bad dreams are usually precipitated by movies, books, or television.

Nine and ten year olds have few fears, but many worries. Most of these worries reinforce the validity of Erikson's theory--that the greatest danger of this period is the development of a sense of inadequacy or inferiority. Eleven-and twelve-year-olds also worry about mastering skills. Additionally, they begin to have concerns about their sexuality.

Anger and fear are closely related emotions. Anger is an outgrowth of frustration and a normal response to restraint, whether physical or psychological. Aggressive behavior may result when gratification is inhibited. This is why a child's anger is often a significant indication of his needs and his emotional life.

Fantasies of six to eight year olds are usually concerned with poorly-resolved oedipal conflicts. In the later stages of latency, sexual wishes, or sexual fantasies, normally manifest positive (heterosexual) or negative (homosexual) strivings toward parent figures. This is considered to be an indication, however subconscious, of sexual drive(s) during the latency period. Daydreaming, or fantasizing about the future, is much more common than actual fantasy. This is a time when children are all-absorbed in real, concrete things and events. Imaginative play and fantasy are minimal at this time.

Myths and fairy tales serve several functions during latency. Fairy tales help a child deal with normal fantasies of developmental conflicts. Myths and fairy tales help children understand cultural limits and expectations. They teach a child how to act in society. Bruno Bettleheim, a noted child psychologist, explains in *The Uses of*

Enchantment: The Meaning and Importance of Fairy Tales[1] that

> In order to master the psychological problems of growing up--
> overcoming narcissistic disappointments, oedipal dilemmas, sibling
> rivalries; becoming able to relinquish childhood dependencies;
> gaining a feeling of selfhood and of self-worth, and a sense of
> moral obligation--a child needs to understand what is going on
> within his conscious self so that he can also cope with that
> which goes on in his unconscious. He can achieve this under-
> standing, and with it the ability to cope, not through rational
> comprehension of the nature and content of his unconscious, but
> by becoming familiar with it through spinning out daydreams--
> ruminating, rearranging, and fantasizing about suitable story ele-
> ments in response to unconscious pressures. By doing this, the
> child fits unconscious content into conscious fantasies, which
> then enable him to deal with that content.

Bettleheim continues with

> It is here that fairy tales have unequaled value, because they
> offer new dimensions to the child's imagination which would be
> impossible for him to discover as truly on his own. Even more
> important, the form and structure of fairy tales suggest images
> to the child; by which he can structure his daydreams and with
> them give better direction to his life.

As children progress from Piaget's stages of intuitive thought
(ages 4-7) to concrete operational thought (7-11), they gain the
ability to distinguish fantasy from reality. This is particularly so
with dreams. Using concrete operational thought, children are able
to perceive that the dream is internal, and produced by their own
thoughts and imagination.

Equally important is the typical flair for dramatization at this
stage. The latency-age child loves to role play: dramatization is a
very effective method for a youngster to explore how other people
think and act and how he should react in turn; it is a significant and
meaningful learning experience.

During middle childhood, humor typically reflects psychosocial
development. Latency is a time of learning, or competence, according
to Erikson. Latency-age children prefer humor that challenges their
intellectual capability. According to Piaget, it is during this period
of concrete operations that children master the concept of reversibility. This ability to mentally reverse operations is necessary to understand the dual meaning of some words. That is why puns, and

---

[1]Bruno Bettleheim, *The Uses of Enchantment: The Meaning and
Importance of Fairy Tales*. (New York: Knopf, 1976), pp. 6-7.

riddles and jokes that "play on words" are universally popular. Elementary school children love to create jingles, tell the latest jokes and riddles over and over again, play practical jokes, and make fun of, or mimic, anyone or anything different.

As children reach the end of middle childhood, significant psychosocial changes emerge. This period, from approximately 10-13, is referred to by various names--prepuberty, postlatency, last stage of latency, and early adolescence. As the physical changes of puberty commence, body prowess becomes a preoccupation in boys. This is often accompanied by a decline in academic interests, and is referred to as the "seventh-grade slump." The redirection of energy into learning--that typifies latency--is now channeled into emerging sexuality. From a psychosexual perspective, castration anxiety is renewed. As puberty begins, humor, too, changes to a sexual orientation. This is a time for jokes about sexual differences and sexual practices. Fierce team loyalty and team spirit replace individual virtuosity.

Girls retain their academic zeal, though they are engrossed with thoughts of menarche and breast development. Interpersonal relationships with friends become intense. The love of horses emerges. This passion for horses has psychosexual connotations. The experience (or fantasy) of riding and "controlling" a powerful animal, while at the same time caring for it and loving it, seems to meet an instinctual bisexual need in girls.

For both sexes, there is a noted resurgence of fantasy. Girls now prefer romance stories and stories about animals, especially horses. Popular topics for boys are, first and foremost, anything relating to sexuality. Boys also enjoy adventure stories and tales of heroism and physical prowess. Boys seem to channel their energies into physically demanding activities and aggressive behavior, while girls channel theirs into incessant talking and imagination.

By the end of the latency period, children should be able to respond to the collective world in terms of concrete operations. They should have developed a sense of industry instead of a sense of inadequacy. Associated tasks are the development of a sense of mastery, peer relationships, moral attitudes and values, and sex role identification. In order for these developmental tasks to be accomplished, parents and teachers must provide support and understanding.

BIBLIOGRAPHY

Bettleheim, Bruno. *The Uses of Enchantment: The Meaning and Importance of Fairy Tales*. New York: Knopf, 1976.

Discusses how fairy tales enable children to understand the deeper meaning in the emotional, sexual, and moral side of their own lives. The author is a child psychiatrist, distinguished for his methods of treating severely emotionally disturbed children. He stresses that children need to make sense out of their own lives before they can appreciate the predicaments of others. Fascinating reading for parents and educators alike.

Bornstein, Berta. "On Latency." *The Psychoanalytic Study of the Child*. New York: International Universities Press, 1951. Volume 6, pp.279-285.

Describes and explains child behavior during the latency period. The author, a child analyst, feels that children this age persistently deny instinctual impulses, and that their partial amnesia for this period may be why grownups remember relatively little about this developmental stage.

Chess, Stella, and Alexander Thomas. *Know Your Child: An Authoritative Guide for Today's Parents*. New York: Basic Books, 1987.

Provides parents--and professionals--with the most comprehensive and interesting information on all aspects of child development and parent-child relations available. Clarifies and consolidates longitudinal research and various theories, while offering warm, practical advice.

Clarke-Stewart, Alison, and Joanne Barbara Koch. *Children: Development through Adolescence*. New York: Wiley, 1983.

Deals with both cognitive and social-emotional development ("head and heart") in the six major developmental periods. Integrates theory and practical application. This book is designed for use as a textbook in introductory courses in child development. Incorporates a glossary, annotated list of suggested readings for each chapter, and extensive references.

Cohen, Dorothy H. *The Learning Child: Guidelines for Parents and Teachers*. New York: Pantheon Books, 1972.

Synthesizes major theories of growth and development and of learning, along with experiences as an educator. Describes the many forces which affect children's learning. Offers parents suggestions on what to do and what not to do to enhance the learning of basic skills, such as reading. Presents constructive criticism on curricula and teaching methods.

Erikson, Erik H. *Childhood and Society.* Second Edition. Revised and Enlarged. New York: Norton, 1963.

The first book by this leading figure in the field of psychoanalysis and human development. It is considered a classic work on the social significance of childhood. Presents his theory on the Eight Stages of Man. Middle Childhood is characterized as the stage of Industry versus Inferiority.

Erikson, Erik H. *Identity: Youth and Crisis.* New York: Norton, 1968.

This book is a successor to *Childhood and Society*, and details the developmental tasks of each stage. It is widely cited for its insights into school-age children and the tasks they must complete to avoid a developmental "identity crisis."

Freud, Sigmund. "Three Essays on the Theory of Sexuality." *The Standard Edition.* London: Hogarth Press, 1953. Volume 7, pp.123-243.

Contains the theories first developed and written by Freud in 1905, describing his theory of Latency and resolution of the Oedipus conflict. This article establishes the basic knowledge of psychosocial development during middle childhood.

Garrison, Carl C., Albert J. Kingston, and Harold W. Bernard. *The Psychology of Childhood: A Survey of Development and Socialization.* New York: Charles Scribner's Sons, 1967.

Takes a biosocial approach to development in middle childhood. Emphasizes the role of family, school, and peers in the socialization process, character development, and personality development. The authors, all college professors, include an annotated bibliography and suggested readings for each chapter.

Gesell, Arnold, Frances L. Ilg, and Louise Bates Ames. *Youth: The Years from Ten to Sixteen.* New York: Harper and Brothers, 1956.

This book, together with the one annotated below, and with *Infant and Child in the Culture of Today: The Guidance of Development*, comprise a classic trilogy of child development literature. Based on firsthand studies of "normal" children, the authors detail the characteristics, behavior patterns, and sequences of development.

Gesell, Arnold, Frances L. Ilg, and Louise Bates Ames. *The Child from Five to Ten.* Revised Edition. Written in collaboration with Glenna E. Bullis. New York: Harper and Row, 1977.

Organizes a year by year series of psychological portraits, with guidance suggestions, of all pertinent areas of development. Includes such topics as emotions, fears and dreams, and interpersonal relations. This revised edition reflects changes in cultural lifestyle and addresses such issues as children and television, and changes in the educational system. This classic book, though still somewhat outdated, provides a wealth of information on child development that is of value to parents, teachers, and all persons concerned with the welfare of children.

Goldings, Herbert J. "Development from Ten to Thirteen Years." *Basic Handbook of Child Psychiatry*. Joseph P. Noshpitz, Editor-in--Chief. Volume 1: Development. New York: Basic Books, 1979, pp. 199-205.

Summarizes and explains the major theories of development regarding physical growth and psychosocial development in prepuberty. Don't let the title intimidate you; *The Basic Handbook of Child Psychiatry* is clearly written, with a minimum of technical jargon. Parents, as well as child care professionals, will find this easy to read and extremely helpful.

Kawin, Ethel. *Early and Middle Childhood*. Volume 2, Parenthood in a Free Nation Series. New York: Macmillan, 1963.

Describes physical, mental and socio-emotional development and relates them to the basic concepts of mature and democratic living. Elaborates on the six essential characteristics of a "mature, responsible citizen" of a free society: (1) Feelings of security and adequacy; (2) Understanding of self and others; (3) Democratic values and goals; (4) Problem-solving attitudes and methods; (5) Self- discipline, responsibility, and freedom; and (6) Constructive attitudes toward change.

Kawin, Ethel. *Later Childhood and Adolescence*. Volume 3, Parenthood in a Free Nation Series. New York: Macmillan, 1963.

Covers the same type of information as Volume 2, but focuses on the preadolescent. This is a non-technical series of books designed primarily to help parents acquire a philosophy of parenthood. Good, basic advice that is essentially timeless.

Maier, Henry W. *Three Theories of Child Development: The Contributions of Erik H. Erikson, Jean Piaget, and Robert R. Sears, and Their Applications*. Revised Edition. New York: Harper and Row, 1969.

Synthesizes, interprets, and compares the Psychoanalytic Theory of Erikson, the Cognitive Theory of Piaget, and the Learning Theory of Sears. Includes an extensive bibliography, suggestions for further reading, and a partial bibliography of these three theorists.

Powell, Gloria Johnson. "Psychosocial Development: Eight to Ten Years." *Basic Handbook of Child Psychiatry.* Joseph P. Noshpitz, Editor-in-Chief. Volume 1: Development. New York: Basic Books, 1979. pp. 190-199.

Reviews the physical, emotional, social, and intellectual development of children at the center of middle childhood. Highlights the psychological landmarks that should be achieved prior to adolescence.

Sarnoff, Charles. *Latency.* New York: Jason Aronson, 1976.

Differentiates the "state" of latency from the latency-age period. Deals with cognitive development, sexuality, superego development, and mechanisms of defense during latency. Written by a child psychotherapist and child analyst as a text for professionals working with children. A valuable handbook encompassing normal development, deviations, and treatment strategies.

Segal, Julius, and Herbert Yahraes. *A Child's Journey: Forces That Shape the Lives of Our Young.* New York: McGraw-Hill, 1978.

Translates the findings of child developmental theorists into a format that reads like an exciting novel. Answers such questions as, "Why do children develop as they do?", "What influences a child's personality and character?", and "What determines the course of a child's mental health?". Written for parents, but also recommended for all adults involved with children.

Solnit, Albert J., Justin D. Call, and Carl B. Feinstein, "Psychosexual Development: Five to Ten Years." *Basic Handbook of Child Psychiatry.* Joseph P. Noshpitz, Editor-in-Chief. Volume 1. New York: Basic Books, 1979. pp.184-190.

Refutes the concept that sexual drives are quiescent during latency. Describes the sequential development of the Oedipal Constellation, and distinguishes between early and late latency. Characterizes the sex differences during latency.

Tribe, Carol. *Profile of Three Theories: Erikson-Maslow-Piaget.* Dubuque, Iowa: Kendall/Hunt, 1982.

Succinctly organizes and presents the essence of these diverse theorists without interpretation or analysis. Utilizes simple language with a minimum of technical jargon. Includes interesting biographical information. Intended as a reference for beginning students of child development.

COGNITIVE DEVELOPMENT DURING MIDDLE CHILDHOOD

The terms cognition and intelligence each have somewhat different meanings, depending on who is doing the defining. Although cognition usually refers to the *process* of learning, and intelligence to the *ability* to learn, they are often used interchangeably. A specific definition of "intelligence" does becomes crucial, however, when attempting any measurement of cognitive functioning.

Significant cognitive development, both quantitatively and qualitatively, occurs during middle childhood. The foremost contributor to our knowledge of intellectual development is Jean Piaget. In fact, to scrutinize cognitive development during middle childhood is to scrutinize Piaget's theories. It is important to keep in mind that Piaget was interested in mental *activity*--what a child *does* in his interaction with his environment, and *how* the child's thought processes evolve. He did not set out to emphasize individual differences in intelligence.

Early in his career, Piaget worked at the Binet Laboratory in Paris, where research was continuing on standardized intelligence tests. Rejecting the quantitative method (based on the number of correct answers on a test) of studying intelligence, he preferred to conduct research into children's thoughts. His method was more flexible. It followed the child's own line of thought, without imposing any direction on it. To Piaget, the study of cognitive development is the study of the *nature* of intelligence, its structure and its functions. He believed that development does not occur as a result of learning. Rather, learning is the result of development.

The Periods of Cognitive Development, according to Piaget, are the sensorimotor period (birth to approximately two years), followed by the preoperational period (approximately 2-7 years). The middle childhood years of 7-11 comprise the period of concrete logical operations, which are, in turn, followed by the formal logical operations period (approximately 11-15 years). Tribe[1] presents the following overview of the concrete logical child:

> (1) The concrete logical child moves intellectually from intuitive thought process to *mental concrete operations.*

---

[1] Carol Tribe, *Profile of Three Theories: Erikson-Maslow-Piaget.* (Dubuque, Iowa: Kendall/Hunt, 1982), p. 104.

(2) He can *decentrate, conserve, reverse action,* and *follow a transition.*

(3) He moves toward an increasing *mastery* of *symbols* and has the freedom to manipulate them as he *plays* with *words* and meanings.

(4) The concrete child is not *egocentric* as the preoperational child is. This child is aware that others can come to conclusions that are different from his. He is *limited* to *concrete, tangible problems* of the present.

(5) The child's *play* is *"interiorized"* in daydreams and enriches intellectual interests and creative thought.

(6) He *shifts models* of *imitation.*

(7) He moves from *external* to *internal moral conscience.*

(8) The child can locate himself in *time,* and learn about *clock, calendar,* and *historical time.*

(9) The child wants to know about the *mechanics of things-- how they work* and how they are made.

(10) The concrete logical child moves from *simple classification* to *multiple classification* and *class inclusion.*

(11) He masters series as the *alphabet* and *number series.*

(12) By the end of the concrete period, he can *add, subtract, multiply, divide, place in order, substitute,* and *reverse.*

Because the writings of Piaget (in French, and in most English translations) are highly technical and thereby difficult to understand, a few definitions of technical terms are in order. *Mental operations* refers to logical thought processes. *Decentrate* means the ability to note several features of an item, such as size, shape and color, along with the interrelationship of those features. *Conservation* is the ability to realize that changing the shape of a material does not change its amount. For example, a cup of water remains eight ounces of water whether it is in a tall, thin cylinder or a short, squat bowl. *Reversibility* is the ability to recognize that every operation can be inverted, as when +1 is inverted to -1, indicating that subtraction is the reverse of addition. *Transition* is the ability to form a mental representation of the relationship between successive items, such as A being larger than B, which is smaller than C, or A>B<C. *Multiple classification* is the simultaneous sorting of objects

based on two or more similar features. It is easy to see why this skill is a prerequisite to the typical hobby of collecting! *Seriation*, the ability to arrange items in order, such as ascending or descending size, is a necessary skill for scientific reasoning. A child must understand the concepts of conservation and seriation before he can understand the number concept. A child must understand *causality* or cause and effect in order to understand *how* things are made and *how* they work. The mastery of these concepts is an essential prerequisite for learning the three R's. Clearly, middle childhood is a critical period for cognitive development!

Still, there are other theories of cognitive development besides those of Piaget. Basically, these are the behavioristic, psychometric, and information-processing theories. They differ primarily in the aspect(s) of intelligence which they emphasize.

Nor do all educators agree with Piaget's theories of cognition, either partially or in total. More recent studies have uncovered exceptions and inconsistencies in his theories. These studies indicate that greater flexibility in age-related stages should be considered. They also suggest that culture, environment, and creativity have a significant influence on cognitive development, particularly during middle childhood. Even though there may be criticisms and challenges to his theory, there is no doubt that Piaget has changed our understanding of children's thinking.

A somewhat different approach to childhood learning is The Montessori Method, an educational system designed to help children learn by themselves. Though usually applied to preschool education, it represents a novel, if not revolutionary, approach to teaching.

Unlike Piaget, Maria Montessori did not believe that human development was hierarchical. Like John Dewey, she believed in the evolutionary context of development, that teaching and/or learning must be based on the needs of growth and of life. Montessori believed that children should be given a "free choice of activity" within a specially "prepared environment," that children prefer work to play, and that there was no need for either rewards or punishment. She emphasized that there are "sensitive periods of development," and that even young children have a profound sense of personal dignity.

It is interesting to note that Maria Montessori was trained as a physician, not as an educator. Initially, she taught mentally defective children, then adapted her method of teaching to preschool children in a slum area of Rome. Later, she travelled throughout the world, writing and lecturing about her teaching method.

Montessori did address the cognitive needs of middle childhood in her writings and her lectures. In her book, *From Childhood to Adolescence*,[2] Montessori states that appropriate learning experiences

---

[2]Maria Montessori, *From Childhood to Adolescence*. (New York: Schocken, 1973), pp 1-10.

for 7-12 year olds should include:

(1) An understanding of what money ought to represent.
(2) The establishment of social relationships outside the school and family.
(3) The need to classify and absorb the outside world via the senses.
(4) Intellectual and moral considerations.
(5) The nourishment of imagination.
(6) The requirement of precision.
(7) The recognition that classification (of details) helps in understanding and aids memory.

Furthermore, Montessori stated that at this age, a child's interest in the world about him naturally leads to inquiries into earth sciences and experimentation and study in organic and inorganic chemistry. An essential principle of Montessori's educational philosophy is that, "To teach details is to bring confusion; to establish the relationship between things is to bring knowledge."[3]

Many experts in education believe that the Montessori Method can help a child become aware of his abilities and gain confidence in himself while making use of his abilities. Supporters of Montessori programs believe that the special materials, used under the guidance of specially trained teachers, help children develop a lasting curiosity and positive attitudes and habits toward learning.

Her critics, on the other hand, contend that the Montessori Method has a tendency to push children into standardized patterns of achievement and to stifle creativity. In addition, they claim that its popularity is due to an emphasis on orderliness, quiet, and obedience which meets the needs of the parents and teachers more than the children's needs. Another criticism is that Montessori's teaching methods were designed to meet the needs of disadvantaged children, such as a Head Start program would, and that such methods are inappropriate for more affluent American students.

Regardless of the validity of such criticism, Montessori has provided education with valuable concepts of how and why children learn, and with an objective approach to the relationship between children and adults in the educational process. Not only do the philosophies of Montessori and Piaget differ; it should be noted that their purposes differ as well. While Montessori sought to promote the application of her concepts to education, Piaget never stressed the practical implications of his work. His concern was to establish a theoretical framework and a research base, not to specify teaching methodology. As such, the two should not be compared; they were not in competition with one another.

----

[3]Ibid., p. 91.

In the past decade, an exciting new approach to the study of thought processes has evolved. This concept is *metacognition*, and it refers to one's knowledge and how one uses, or applies, that knowledge. Most of the research into metacognition has come from the field of cognitive psychology. It is a somewhat confusing concept because it is often difficult to distinguish between cognition and metacognition.

Nevertheless, research into metacognition offers the possibility of greater understanding of the strategies involved in the development of language and memory, perception, attention, comprehension learning, communication, and problem solving. The importance of metacognition and its potential impact on educational strategies is so great that Chess and Thomas[4] offer this caveat for parents:

> The research activities in metacognition promise to lead to evidence that training in the process of thinking may succeed in raising a child's ability to do higher order thinking. If so, individuals or groups will undoubtedly appear, as they have for the IQ and other issues, with claims that they have simple, guaranteed methods for teaching metacognition. When this happens, parents should be very wary of such claims, investigate them thoroughly, and get the judgement of competent professionals before pushing their child into such programs.

A child uses different cognitive skills for math than he does for reading. Mathematical principles are based on concrete, pliable materials, and are therefore well suited for kindergarten. The same cannot be said for reading, which differs significantly in cognitive requirements and from the child's natural learning style. This difference is clearly illustrated by Dorothy Cohen[5] of the Bank Street College of Education in New York.

> Imagine a child of 5, 6, or 7 standing before a balance scale trying to match a pound of toothpicks on one side with a pound of nails on the other. Out of his efforts, physical in character, he comes to recognize that there is no relation between volume and weight. This is sound mathematical thinking, which serves as the base for an *eventual* symbolic rendering of questions. Developed out of first-hand experience, it has far more meaning

---

[4]Stella Chess and Alexander Thomas, *Know Your Child: An Authoritative Guide for Today's Parents*. (New York: Basic Books, 1987), p. 153.

[5]Dorothy H. Cohen, *The Learning Child: Guidelines for Parents and Teachers*. (New York: Pantheon, 1972), p. 75.

to a child than if it had been learned by rote.

Cohen continues with

> But reading is a symbolic system to begin with which must
> be learned before meaning can be abstracted. And the symbols
> bear no relationship to anything concrete and real as they do in
> math. Before a child can learn to use the symbols of reading,
> he must grasp the existence of symbol systems as such, and find
> a quality of reality in an abstraction. However, to "see" the
> meaning of reading, a child can do almost nothing by himself.
> Only as and if he listens while countless stories are read to
> *him,* countless labels interpreted for *him,* and countless signs
> explained to *him,* does the essential meaning of symbols in print
> become clear to him.... It is true that children can be helped to
> memorize the letters of the alphabet by concrete approaches
> such as sandpaper letters or tracing letters. But *recognizing*
> the basic tools is hardly the same as learning the principles
> which the skill supports.... Learning to read involves three
> stages: (1) Awareness that print conveys meaning, (2) Remem-
> bering/recognizing a word as a unit, and (3) Analysis of how
> words look and sound.

In learning basic skills, rote memory is of little value. True
learning cannot be hurried; it develops in sequential stages. For example, the ability to count has little relation to an understanding of
mathematics. Likewise, being able to recite the alphabet does not
indicate reading readiness. A child must first reach a developmental
level that is consistent with understanding the necessary concepts
and the symbols. Physiological maturation, especially of the central
nervous system, is essential for cognitive growth.

Piaget recognized that children could not be taught to function
beyond their developmental level. He believed that the normal,
everyday interaction of children with their physical environment was
crucial for cognitive growth. He is quoted as warning

> Be careful not to push children beyond their cognitive level.
> Children think with their brains, they can only think with the
> neural connections that have developed at that particular time.
> Hurrying a child through a stage will not speed up brain growth.
> It will only deprive a child of the proper experiences needed for
> stimulation.[6]

Parents who do not recognize the futility of "cognitive stimulation"

---

[6]Margaret Boden, *Jean Piaget*. (New York: Viking Press, 1980),
p. 66.

are vulnerable prey to those who promote programmed curricula and books which claim to advance children's cognition beyond their age-level. Trying to "teach a two-year old to read" is not the way to ensure being the parent of a gifted child! A common characteristic of many gifted children is that they come from homes where one or both parents have a great love of learning. To enhance the development of intelligence, parents should avoid formal training schemes and instead, talk to their children; answer their questions; read to them; take them on trips to the country, to parks, zoos, and museums. Children learn by their experiences. In middle childhood, they are natural explorers and investigators. They learn math and science by "hands on" experiments. They have open minds and learn best as active participants. They learn vocabulary by observing how the words are used in meaningful contexts. Children master skills in reading and mathematics at their own individual rate. The pressure of time, grades, and competition hinders, rather than helps the process.

Obviously, a child's environment has a profound influence on all aspects of his development. Heredity must be considered as well, for there is a continuous, reciprocal interaction between hereditary and environmental factors. Heredity establishes the parameters of a child's intelligence; environment can maximize or minimize a child's potential within those parameters. A child's intelligence is the product of both biological-hereditary and environmental factors. It is not feasible to ascertain which factor is more influential; there are too many variables possible.

Much controversy, and even confusion, exist on the issue of Intelligence Tests, commonly referred to as IQ Tests. Even though such tests are designed to measure several primary mental abilities, the IQ score is expressed in terms of general intelligence. The IQ test consists of separate subtests that rate a child's knowledge, comprehension of meaning of words, abstract thinking, and ability to reason. Each subtest is scored on a rating system in the which the average child's performance is 100. The final IQ is then obtained by averaging the sum of all the subtest scores, multiplied by 100, and then divided by the subject's chronological age. The IQ subscores are divided into verbal and performance groups; the full IQ is obtained by averaging these two groups.

Actually, the IQ measures only a part of the intelligence. It measures the ability to learn abstract and verbal subject matter in school. It does not measure practical or mechanical ability or the ability to deal with people, or musical ability, art ability, or any of the hosts of other types of function that require intelligence of other sorts. Nor does the IQ test measure the emotional or other personality factors that might interfere with the utilization of one's ability. A child's score on an intelligence test is a measure of how many exercises and problems he can complete correctly. The number of items he can complete correctly depends upon hereditary characteristics, opportunity for learning, physical, mental, and emotional conditions, and motivation.

According to Chess and Thomas,[7] the IQ test has value *if* we recognize its limitations. Test scores *may* be indicative of certain aspects of a child's intellectual functioning, they *may* be predictive of later academic achievement, and they *may* be helpful in identifying whether a school problem is caused by intellectual functioning or not. If a problem is detected in a particular area of functioning, then remedial measures can be instituted.

One weakness which Chess and Thomas cite is that a child may perform poorly due to inadequate instructions or to an impersonal manner on the part of the tester. The child may be confused about the meaning of the test, or he may have minimal experience with the content of one or more of the subtests, or even the language in which the test is administered. He may have a perceptual problem, or may just be resistant to taking this or any test.

Other problems include the cultural bias of the test. They feel that there is no such thing as a culture-free test for any charac-teristic or trait. Also, a poor score can lead to a self-fulfilling prophesy. Since the social implications of a low IQ score can be devastating, Chess and Thomas caution that before labeling a child, it is imperative to evaluate the testing procedure, and retest under more favorable circumstances.

Alternatives to the IQ test are tests which give credit for cor-rect answers given with the help of the examiner, and tests which measure general competence rather than general intelligence. A fur-ther discussion of tests and testing is to be found in the chapter, *The Elementary School Experience*.

The relationship of creativity and giftedness to intelligence is the subject of much debate and research. True creativity is a gift that is not measurable. In fact, a gifted child may score low in IQ. Creative children tend to be nonconformists, have a strong sense of self-direction, are open to creative ideas, show great persistence, and have a great appreciation of humor even though they may not evi-dence a sense of humor.

There are two types of gifted children, or children with excep-tional talent. One is the child with generally high intelligence who displays a particular talent in some specific field. The other is the child who does not manifest high intelligence outside of the area of his special talent. Exceptional talent without generalized ability may possibly have a neurological or physiological origin, perhaps of a he-reditary nature. Musical talent is a good example of this theory. Other possible reasons include focusing on the talent to the exclusion of other aspects of development. This narrowing of development may be fostered by the parents or by the child's own drive or both.

---

[7]Ibid., p. 261.

Children who are gifted in abstract thinking will usually excel in math, science, and chess. Children gifted in music have a similar affinity for abstraction, but also require keen auditory acuity.

An appreciation of normal growth and development is essential in understanding how children learn. Children are more likely to develop to their potential if they have parents who are supportive and teachers who provide appropriate educational experiences.

BIBLIOGRAPHY

Chess, Stella, and Alexander Thomas. *Know Your Child: An Authoritative Guide for Today's Parents.* New York: Basic Books, 1987.

Presents sound information not only on intelligence, but also on cognitive stimulation, cognition and metacognition, the value and dangers of IQ tests, and alternatives to IQ tests as well.

Clarke-Stewart, Alison, and Joanne Barbara Koch. *Children: Development through Adolescence.* New York: Wiley, 1983.

Consolidates the historical background, theories, and methodology of contemporary developmental psychology. Presents a comprehensive overview of how intelligence develops, how it is tested, variations in development, cognitive styles, creativity, and family influence. An introductory text for courses in child development that includes many instructional aids and references.

Cohen, Dorothy H. *The Learning Child: Guidelines for Parents and Teachers.* New York: Pantheon, 1972.

Discusses at length the styles of growth and learning, and how each affects reading, writing, and mathematics. Cohen stresses that an appreciation/understanding of normal growth and development is an essential prerequisite to understanding cognitive development. Emphasizes that individual differences may affect learning. Minimizes the controversy over phonics; states that 70% of children will learn to read by either method. Points out the special difficulties in learning to read English versus other languages. Offers advice to parents, such as not insisting that a child "sound out" a word, and how to be good listeners to their child's reading.

Donaldson, M. *Children's Minds.* Glasgow: Collins, 1978.

Donaldson's thesis is that young children's powers of reasoning are far more developed than Piaget's interpretation suggests. Examines why children fail at school.

Durkin, Delores. *Children Who Read Early: Two Longitudinal Studies.* New York: Teachers College Press, 1966.

Reports the first major research study on the who, how, why, and when of reading readiness. Concludes that nothing is to be gained by an early start. Though written over two decades ago, has significance today with the current emphasis on teaching children skills at an early age.

Gardner, Howard. *Frames of Mind*. New York: Basic Books, 1985.

Proposes the measurement of seven multiple competencies/intel-ligences (linguistic, musical, logical-mathematical, spatial, bodily kinesthetic, interpersonal, and intrapersonal) as an alternative to IQ testing.

Ginsburg, Herbert, and Sylvia Opper. *Piaget's Theory of Intellectual Development: An Introduction*. Englewood Cliffs, N.J.: Prentice Hall, 1969.

Presents the basics of Piaget's ideas in clear and concise language. Intended for undergraduate students of Piagetian theory. Considers Piaget's major theoretical notions concerning intellectual development, such as symbolism, communication, thought content, moral judgement, reasoning, classification, and conservation, as well as some of the research on which they are based. The book concludes with a discussion of genetic epistemology and the implications of Piaget's ideas for educational practice.

Glover, John A. *A Parents Guide to Intelligence Testing: How to Develop Your Children's Intellectual Development*. Chicago: Nelson Hall, 1979.

A book for parents who would like to know more about the significance of the scores their children received on intelligence tests and how to interpret those scores in relation to the child. Written by an associate professor of educational psychology at the University of Nebraska, this book discusses four general areas: (1) General information concerning the use and interpretation of intelligence tests; (2) Reasons why scores on intelligence tests may be inordinately high or low; (3) What parents can do to enhance the mental abilities in their children that are measured by intelligence tests; and (4) Relationship of creativity to intelligence and the measurement and development of creative abilities in children.

Graves, Ruth, ed. *The RIF* Guide to Encouraging Young Readers*. Garden City, N.Y.: Doubleday, 1987.

RIF (Reading is Fun-damental) is a twenty-year-old nonprofit organization associated with the Smithsonian Institute that is dedicated to encouraging the art and joy of reading, particularly aimed at disadvantaged children. This new publication is a sourcebook of fun activities, all related to books and reading. It contains an annotated list of books for children to grow on and resources for parents and children.

Healy, Jane M. *Your Child's Growing Mind: A Parents Guide to Learning from Birth to Adolescence.* Garden City, N.Y.: Doubleday, 1987.

Presents background information on the biology of children's brains. Describes how language and academic learning develop. Discusses intelligence and memory. Advises parents on constructive ways to help their children learn, while cautioning them on providing too much help. The author, a learning specialist, issues a scathing indictment of early pressures to read, and scientifically refutes the "superbaby" myth. A general bibliography is included, as well as a selected bibliography for each chapter.

Hunt, J. McV. *Intelligence and Experience.* New York: Ronald Press, 1961.

Examines the historical roots of the assumptions of fixed intelligence and of pre-determined development. Reviews the research on the role of experience in the development of intelligence. A classic reference text for teachers and educators.

Isaacs, Nathan. *A Brief Introduction to Piaget: The Growth of Understanding in the Young Child; New Light on Children's Ideas of Numbers.* New York: Shocken Books, 1961.

Relates Piaget's notions of numbers, space, movement and time in an understandable format. The author, known as a leading critic and interpreter of Piaget, calls attention to and clarifies common misunderstandings of Piaget's work.

Kohl, Herbert. *Basic Skills: A Plan for Your Child, A Program for All Children.* New York: Bantam, 1982.

Addresses a primary concern in education today. Of special interest is the section on the relationship between mechanical skills and the content of what is learned, and the appendix on testing. Stresses the correct use of testing and the negative consequences of standardized testing. An extensive bibliography is included.

Levinger, Leah. "The Child with Exceptional Talent." *Basic Handbook of Child Psychiatry.* Joseph P. Noshpitz, Editor-in-Chief. Volume 1. New York: Basic Books, 1979. pp. 334-338.

Explores the various theories about the evolution and adaptation of exceptionally talented or gifted children. The reference list is both broad and useful.

Montessori, Maria. *From Childhood to Adolescence.* New York: Schocken Books, 1973. (Translated from the French by the Montessori Educational Research Center.)

Focuses on the characteristics and needs of children from 7-12, showing that when a special environment is provided, they are able and eager to apply themselves to fields of study usually reserved for high school students. A compilation of the controversial ideas and theories of this pioneering educator. This is one of the few books by or about Montessori that deals with middle childhood.

Mussen, Paul H., ed. *Handbook of Child Psychology*. Fourth Edition. Volume III: *Cognitive Development*, John H. Flavel and Ellen M. Markman, volume editors. New York: John Wiley and Sons, 1983.

A technical source book on the state of the art and the current knowledge, formerly published as *Carmichael's Manual of Child Psychology*. Reflects the changes in child psychology since 1970, including information on metacognition, and reinterpretations on the work of Jean Piaget.

Piaget, Jean. *Six Psychological Studies*. Introduction, notes, and glossary by David Elkind, Translation from the French by Anita Tenzer, and Translation edited by David Elkind. New York: Vintage, 1968.

This title is misleading; this book is an easy-to-read introduction to Piaget's multidisciplinary theories on intelligence. Details the stages in the mental development of children. Children from seven to twelve are discussed in terms of behavior, thought progression, operational thinking, affectivity, will, and moral feelings.

Pulaski, Mary Ann Spencer. *Understanding Piaget: An Introduction to Children's Cognitive Development*. New York: Harper and Row, 1971.

Reviews the theoretical rationale behind Piaget's work and sets forth his basic principles of development. Highlights the impact of Piaget's views on education, teacher training, and psychology. Discusses measures for implementing Piaget's concepts in the classroom and teacher training. Glossary and bibliography.

Pyle, David W. *Intelligence: An Introduction*. London: Routledge and Kegan Paul, 1979.

The author, a teacher and educator in England, examines such topics as, "What is intelligence?", "Can it be measured?", and "What affects intelligence?". Recommended especially for educators concerned with the developmental disabilities of children. Contains an extensive bibliography, and annotated suggestions for further reading.

Standing, Edward Mortimer. *Maria Montessori: Her Life and Work*. New York: Mentor Books, 1962.

Provides a biographical glimpse into the life of this famous educator whose ideas have challenged and revolutionized teaching concepts. Presents her thoughts in the context of the evolution of the Montessori schools.

FAMILY INTERACTIONS DURING MIDDLE CHILDHOOD

The family is the basic unit of life's experiences. The interactions within a family, whether they directly involve the child or not, contribute to the personality of the child, and his ability to function in society. A child's emotional well-being cannot be evaluated in isolation from his family unit.

Within any family unit that includes children, there are three avenues of interaction--the one between parents, the one between parents and children, and the one between siblings. Children have minimal influence upon the content and quality of the parental interaction, although the parental interaction has a major influence upon the children. Parental interaction is largely shaped by the personalities of the parents themselves, environmental influences, and the degree of satisfaction parents perceive in their individual role(s) in life. The manner in which parents interact and express their love for each other and for their children establishes the emotional climate of the family.

Parent-child interaction changes as children grow and become more independent. Parents will often relate to their children (and to each other) according to the patterns of their own families of origin. In the early years of middle childhood, the parent is usually seen as omnipotent by the child, and the parent's authority is rarely questioned. As the child approaches adolescence, he rejects the standards of his parents as part of the developmental process of establishing his own identity.

Sibling interaction is shaped by the parents and by society. If parents encourage competition and show favoritism among children, sibling rivalry often intensifies. Our culture emphasizes individuality and independence. In other cultures, the needs of the family are stressed above the needs of the individual child. In a traditional Mexican family, for example, older children look after younger siblings, and are fiercely protective and caring towards them.

Children are significantly influenced by their siblings. While sibling interaction can be one of rivalry and envy, it can also promote development through acceptance, friendliness, cooperation, loyalty, and positive role identifications. Even though siblings have the same biological parents, each has his own genetic makeup and individual temperament. Sibling interaction is affected by birth order, the spacing of siblings, and family size.

The family serves many functions in this or any society. These functions are both biological and sociological. The traditional family still constitutes a majority in American life, yet there are many alternative forms of families today. The fact that they are different does not mean that they are inferior. Many of us nostalgically associate "family" with the nuclear family in which father worked, and mother stayed home to take care of the children. To others, "family" evokes memories of a more extended family relationship, in which grandparents, godparents, and other relatives and close friends all helped out in childrearing. In fact, parents of today will often admit that they feel inadequate because the roles of being a husband or a wife or a parent have changed so much from the days when they were kids. The child psychiatrist Alvin Poussaint,[1] says of parenting roles, "The mores of one's culture, religious orientation, country, community, and family influence the kind of role a mother and father assume in child-raising."

Today there are many families headed by a parent who is single either by choice, death, or divorce. As divorces and remarriages have increased, so have the number of step-families, or families in which there are "his, hers, and theirs" children. The composition may vary, but the family's role is still that of provider, housekeeper, child care, child socialization, therapeutic, sexual, recreational, and kinship.

It is interesting to observe how children who are affected by these changing roles define families. This question was posed to children and their answers compiled in *The Kids' Book about Single-Parent Families: By Kids for Everyone*:[2]

> Everybody's family is different. A family can be any group of people who love each other. They don't have to live together, and they don't even really have to be related. A group of people can just decide to become a family. Some families have kids and some don't... Just having two parents who live together won't make it perfect. Every kid needs something different from a family, and as long as you can get love and security from your family, that will be enough.

Still, these rapid changes in family structure have increased the level of stress for parents and children alike, and have prompted some social scientists to predict the demise of the family. In a *New*

---

[1]Bill Cosby, *Fatherhood*. Introduction and afterword by Alvin F. Poussaint, M.D. (Garden City, NY: Doubleday, 1986), in afterword.

[2]Paul Dolmetsch and Alexa Shih, eds., *The Kids' Book about Single-Parent Families: By Kids for Everyone*. (New York: Doubleday), 1985.

York Times article[3] a decade ago, Urie Bronfenbrenner of Cornell University cited divorce statistics, the number of single-parent families, working mothers, the rise of juvenile delinquency and illegitimate births as evidence that the family was in desperate decline. Other experts quoted these dynamic trends[4] (in 1977):

(1) The divorce rate has doubled in the last 10 years.

(2) It is estimated that two out of every five children born in this decade will live in single-parent homes for at least part of their youth.

(3) The number of households headed by women has increased by more than a third in this decade, has more than doubled in one generation.

(4) More than half of all mothers with school-age children now work outside the home, as do more than a third of mothers with children under the age of 3.

(5) One out of every three schoolchildren lives in a home headed by only one parent or relative.

(6) Day care of irregular quality is replacing the parental role in many working families. Similarly, there has been extraordinary growth in the classifications that sociologists call "latchkey children"--children unsupervised for portions of the day, usually in the period between the end of school and a working parent's return home.

(7) The average number of children per family has dropped from a recent high of 3.8 in 1957 to 2.04 today, meaning a further constriction of the natural nuclear family, but an expansion of legal kinships through divorce and remarriage.

Other social scientists disagreed, taking a more upbeat view that a changing world mandates changing institutions, and that the family is responding positively to change by developing new forms within the basic structure. They argued that well-adjusted parents and resilient children could handle the emotional impact of changing family structures.

Regardless of the statistics, the experts, and the predictions, the reality is that family structure *is* changing, and that, as a result, many parents have less time to spend with their children. Even so, parents must realize that it is the *quality* of the time spent in parent-child interactions, not the *quantity* which makes the difference!

One of the most positive changes in parent-child interactions

---

[3]Jon Nordheimer, "The Family in Transition: A Challenge from Within," *The New York Times*, November, 27, 1977, pp. 1 and 74.

[4]Ibid.

has been the increased involvement of fathers in all aspects of their children's care. Nowadays, fathers attend Lamaze classes along with their expectant mate, provide emotional support during delivery, and share in meeting the infant's physical needs. Their children are growing up with a non-sexist view of the role of a father in family relationships. Most studies indicate that the children in such households are well-adjusted and have fewer problems with their own sex-role identity.

Parental jobs often require frequent travel which further limits the quantity of parent-child interaction. There are ways, however, to improve the quality of available interactions, based on the developmental stage and need of the child. Bettie Youngs, author of *Stress in Children*,[5] says it helps to understand first why even a busy child seems to fret when a parent is away. "Children fear the unknown," Youngs said. "They dearly love their parents. And when they don't know exactly what is happening, they start fantasizing."

Thus it is important, Youngs said, to leave "a trail of access" every time. This might take the form of a chat in advance to explain where you are going and what you will be doing, followed by a written itinerary that lets the child know where you can be reached every day.

Working mothers, especially those working by choice, often find that interaction with their children has improved. These women gain self-confidence and broaden their interests by working outside the home. Society no longer stigmatizes the woman who works, even if she has a husband who earns a good living. In fact, there is increased social pressure on housewives today to find work and not to be dependent on their husbands.

Children of working mothers do very well *if* the mother is satisfied with her work, and if the mother receives sufficient support, especially from the father. It is also crucial that high quality substitute child care be available, and that the mother maintain sufficient energy and time for her family. Working mothers provide a positive role model for their daughters, according to a *New York Times Magazine*[6] article

Studies suggest that independent and achieving mothers engender similar qualities in their daughters, and that these daughters have higher career aspirations and greater self-esteem than daughters of non-working mothers. Child specialists also believe that as more children grow up in families of working mothers, both boys and girls will find it easier to balance their

[5]Bettie Youngs, *Stress in Children*. (New York: Avon), 1987.

[6]Anita Shrive, "The Working Mother as Role Model," *New York Times Magazine*, September 9, 1984, pp. 39-54.

masculine and feminine characteristics than their parents did.

The article concludes by quoting Lawrence Balter of New York University:

> Psychiatric theories lag behind social reality. Changing them requires a new generation. People will have to rethink the old. We are on the threshold of that thinking.

Parent-child interactions can also suffer when a mother works. Such interaction-problems develop when children are given inappropriate freedoms/responsibilities, or when the children are expected to achieve beyond their limits. As example, single parents or families in which both parents work often use packaged programs, advertised to advance learning, in the as-yet unproven expectation that these will promote their children's maturity, while at the same time keeping the children occupied. They rationalize that it's for the child's own good.

The term "latchkey children" typifies what is meant by imparting inappropriate freedom/responsibility to children. These are children in middle childhood who are left alone and unsupervised from the end of the school day until the parent returns home from work, usually about 5:30 P.M. In the summer of 1987, a telephone survey of parent and teacher concerns was conducted for the Metropolitan Life Insurance Company.[7] The majority of teachers questioned said that isolation and lack of supervision after school was the major reason children have difficulty in school. The study theorized that not doing well in school was a manifestation of the children's preoccupation with taking care of themselves. It cautioned against asking children to be responsible for themselves at too young an age and for too long a period of time. This problem of asking children to give up their childhood right to be dependent cut across all economic lines and rural, suburban, and urban boundaries.

There is a need to provide after-school programs for children of working parents. Most parents would prefer to have these programs organized by the schools, and have them provide recreational or extra-curricular activities rather than just educational programs. Some organizations offer special telephone lines in an attempt to provide some sense of security to children alone and frightened after school. Parent-child interaction can suffer, however, when agencies meet the needs and functions that the family traditionally provided.

One way for working parents to prevent negative patterns of parent-child interaction is to create special high quality time with a child to compensate for parental absence. High quality time is that

---

[7]Metropolitan Life Insurance Company, *The American Teacher 1987: Strengthening Links between Home and School*. New York, 1987.

in which the parent and child are interactively engaged with each other in a warm and accepting manner that promotes a child's intellectual, social, or emotional development.

Relationships with grandparents and other kinship ties are a vital link in all aspects of family interaction. Grandparents provide a sense of continuity with the past, and a source of cultural heritage. They can be an invaluable support in time of family crisis. Relatives can also help give a child a sense of security, of belonging, and of identity.

Divorce is a major issue that affects all family interactions. The impact of divorce on children may differ according to the child's age, sex, developmental level, the emotional availability of each parent, and post-divorce consequences for the child. Regardless of the circumstances, the loss of a parent through divorce is highly stressful for children. Indeed, children are the ones who suffer most in bad marriages and bitter divorces.

During middle childhood especially, the pain of family stress in a divorce can profoundly affect a child. Seven-to nine-year-olds may become depressed, immobilized by their suffering, and vulnerable to regression. Early latency is an age when children depend on their parents for a role model, and much of their own self-concept depends on the approval or disapproval of their parents. Children this age tend to interpret the divorce of their parents as a rejection of themselves, in contrast to the preschooler thinking himself to be the cause of the divorce. In their emotional immaturity, they feel their survival threatened. Anger, fear, betrayal, and deprivation are common, yet the overriding emotion is that of persistent sadness. Their sense of loss is akin to the grief of death. Boys are particularly devastated by the loss of their father. Boys and girls both need frequent attention from the absent parent and assurances that although the family structure has changed, they still belong to a family that cares about them.

Towards the end of middle childhood, the profound sadness occasioned by divorce evolves into a sense of anger towards the parents. The breakdown of parent-child interaction that usually accompanies divorce only exacerbates the problem. Often, these children are given adult responsibilities before they can handle them, or they are placed in the role of confidant and advisor to the parents. Too often, children are placed in the middle of their parents' hostility, and are confused about how to communicate with each without being disloyal. They don't understand their parents' feelings. Children need to talk about these feelings, and many schools find that peer group discussions can help to ameliorate the problem.

Relationships between mother and children, especially sons, can become strained in a divorce when the non-custodial father is overly permissive and indulgent with the child, or when the idealized father is constantly berated by the mother. It is normal for children to identify with the absent parent of the same sex, and children therefore interpret the rejection of that parent as a rejection of themselves. It is understandably stressful for children to love two people who seem to hate each other.

When children don't understand something, they tend to fantasize about it. This is especially true of divorce. It is difficult for parents to discuss their true feelings with their children. Parental feelings may involve emotions that are incomprehensible to children. Latency-age children operate in a world of concrete, not abstract thoughts. Parental reconciliation and reunion is a frequent fantasy of divorced children. Like all children, they need and seek security in their lives. Positive parent-child interaction during the stress of divorce can do much to ameliorate negative effects on the child. The support of peers, family friends, and relatives is also of great comfort and assistance to children of divorce. Many children report their siblings to be the major source of support during a divorce.

Following divorce, a child's family is re-formed into a single-parent family, or at some future date into a stepfamily unit. As the constellation of the child's family changes, new avenues of interaction are often required. If the child becomes part of a stepfamily, all members assume new or different roles. There will be a new parent-to-parent interaction, a new sibling-interaction if the stepparent has children, and a different parent-child interaction. At the same time, the child may still have a relationship with the non-custodial parent, and the original sibling relationship may continue. The establishment of new family-interaction patterns can be stressful for all concerned. Discipline, divided loyalty, and visitation with the absent parent are often issues of discord.

The manner in which a parent becomes a single parent is of great importance. If death or divorce is the cause, that parent will have gone through a major life crisis--the loss of a spouse. In addition to coping with that loss, the single parent is usually confronted with concerns about finances, employment, day care, and social life. If divorce is the cause, there may also be pressures from the former spouse and his family. If the single parent remarries, there are adjustment problems to be worked out in a stepfamily situation. There are many reasons why a single or remarried parent may not be as emotionally available to his children as the children desire or need. These reasons are bound to affect the quality of the parent-child interaction.

A stepfamily has its own patterns, strengths, and challenges. Stepfamilies are a growing phenomenon in our society. According to a *New York Times* report on a stepfamily conference,[8] it is estimated that there are now 11 million families in which at least one spouse has been married before. This is an increase from 8.9 million in

---

[8]Glenn Collins, "80's Stepfamilies: Forming New Ties," *The New York Times*, September 24, 1987, pp. C 1 and C 10.

in 1970, and the number includes the family of the nation's President. About 5 million families in this group have children under the age of 18. It is anticipated that one child in four will become a stepchild before reaching the age of 18. There is even a designated Stepparent's Day which is now observed in five states on the first Sunday in October. Although conference attendees did not like the term stepfamily, they liked alternatives, such as "blended family" and "reconstructed family," even less.

Parent-child relationships may also differ somewhat in the case of adopted children. Adopted children are usually born out of wedlock, adopted through agencies, and learn of their adoption at about age three. Their adjustment and family relationship usually depends on how each reacts to the adoption. The latency-age child is able to understand a factual account of his adoption, and truthfulness can promote a positive parent-child interaction. Negative reactions of the child result when he feels that he doesn't measure up to the parent's expectations, or that he was given away because he was undesirable. Parents react negatively to their adopted child if they feel guilty about being unable to conceive, or if they are concerned about undesirable hereditary traits of the biological parents. As with all parents who desperately want children, they often find it hard to set limits for them. Information about the biological parents will help to prevent the child from fantasies that often idealize the biological parents and deprecate the adoptive parents.

Each home and each family may be said to be unique. Each has a personality all its own that includes the patterns of interactions, the standards, beliefs, and attitudes, the parental authority patterns, and the emotional ties. The core of any child's sense of security, indeed of his world, lies in his family.

Most families succeed in providing this. Its importance is emphasized by its absence in the all too poignant story, presented by a recent letter to the *New York Times*,[9] evoked in response to an article on improving the city schools

.... The core of the problem is the home, or rather no home. I have been teaching skills in a technical school for seven years. My students are at the "last chance hotel." They are 18 to 27 years old, and many are also getting their general education diplomas at the same time....

In an average class of 27, three-quarters have high blood pressure and sometimes remember to take their medication. Three-quarters have never seen their father, and most of the women have a love-hate relationship with men. All, male and female, have one or more children they take to a day-care cen-

---

[9]Jean L. Banks, "School Problems Start Long before Children Enter a Classroom," *The New York Times*, September 12, 1987.

ter before school. All work before or after school. They get minimum sleep.

Half have been burned out of their homes once. All are on welfare. Most have children with high lead counts, allergies and chronic bronchitis. Most have been sexually molested or raped by friends or relatives. All know someone who died a violent death or was stabbed or shot. Some have been mugged and their apartments burglarized. I would say most have had traumatized childhoods.

Can you educate that mind in that body? Let's start at the beginning with the most basic primal need, an apartment to come home to, a kitchen table to do homework on, a mother and father.

BIBLIOGRAPHY

Ackerman, Nathan W. *The Psychodynamics of Family Life: Diagnosis and Treatment of Family Relationships*. New York: Basic Books, 1958.

This book is a classic on family psychodynamics. It was written by the founder of the Ackerman Institute in New York City, a training and treatment center for family therapy. Presents information on the family as a unit, and how various members interact. Ackerman believes that a child cannot be viewed in isolation from his family and environment, that all are closely interrelated. The role of family in the emotional development of the child is paramount. Suggests ways to evaluate a child's behavior within the context of family interactions.

Berg, Barbara J. *The Crisis of the Working Mother: Resolving the Conflict between Family and Work*. New York: Summit, 1986.

Deals with the guilt, the crucial salaries, the conflicts, the competing demands, and the feelings of the working mother. Offers encouragement and psychological insights.

Berman, Claire. *Making It as a Stepparent: New Roles, New Rules*. Garden City, N.Y.: Doubleday, 1980.

Explores all angles of the stepfamily situation, from the role of finances to the confusion of merging two or more different lifestyles. A realistic look at how and why stepparenting is different from primary parenting. This book is based on interviews with hundreds of remarried women, men, and their children.

Bettleheim, Bruno. *A Good Enough Parent: A Book on Child-Rearing*. New York: Knopf, 1987.

Presents the thesis that parents must not indulge their impulse to create the child they would *like* to have, but instead help their child develop fully--in his own good time--into the person that he wishes to be and can become. Written by a preeminent child psychologist, this book offers practical ways for parents to avoid stressful relationships with their children.

Bloom-Fishbach, Jonathan, Sally Bloom-Fishbach, and Associates. *The Psychology of Separation and Loss*. San Francisco: Jossey-Bass, 1987.

Examines how the experiences of separation and loss, such as work-related separation and divorce, influence development in childhood.

Brazelton, T. Berry. *Working and Caring*. Reading, Mass.: Addison-Wesley, 1985.

Offers support and reassurance along with sound, practical advice and suggestions that cover the many exigencies that may arise. Stresses that many people and situations influence the developmental process. Discusses the "goodness of fit" concept, which he defines as a good match between the parent's attitudes and expectations and the child's temperament and other characteristics. Brazelton profiles three families (Professional; blue-collar; and single working mother) and how they deal with their dual roles as parents and workers.

Capaldi, Frederick, and McRae, Barbara. *Step-Families: A Cooperative Responsibility*. New York: Vision Books, 1979.

Deals with the practical issues faced by single parents, natural parents, absentee parents, and their children. This book is brief and easy to read, offering guidelines along with information about legal issues, adoption, and finances.

Caplow, Theodore; H. M. Bahr; B.A. Chadwick; R. Hill; and M. H. Willamson. *Middletown Families: Fifty Years of Change and Continuity*. Minneapolis: University of Minnesota Press, 1982.

Based on the research of the *Middletown III* Project, 1976-81, under a grant from the National Science Foundation. Authors have duplicated the original studies, done in 1924-25, and again in 1935, to gauge the changes that have taken place in a typical American town in the last 50 years. *Middletown Families* explores such issues as changing family roles, effects of women working, sexual attitudes, parent-child relations, and kinship ties. Contrary to predictions, evidence points to stronger families, closer bonds, increased tolerance, and greater marital satisfaction than 50 years previous.

Dizenhuz, Israel. "Children and Divorce." *Basic Handbook of Child Psychiatry*. Joseph P. Noshpitz, Editor-in-Chief. Volume 1. New York: Basic Books, 1979. pp.378-382.

Explains how the loss of a parent by divorce differs from loss by death, primarily because of the power of the court and the adversarial nature of the legal processes involved. Details the effect on children in different stages of development.

Dodson, Fitzhugh. *How to Single Parent*. New York: Harper and Row, 1987.

Advises how to cope with the pressure of being a single parent. Deals with custody and visitation issues, dating, sex and marriage. By the author of *How to Parent* and *How to Father*.

Dolmetsch, Paul, and Alexa Shih, eds. *The Kids' Book about Single-Parent Families: By Kids for Everyone*. Garden City, N.Y.: Doubleday, 1985.

Written by kids 11-15 to send the message that, "For kids in single-parent families everything is not going to be the same, but it will be all right." Contains interesting list of pros and cons from the kids' points of view. Includes reviews of books about divorce and single-parent families.

Faber, Adele, and Elaine Mazlich. *Sibling Rivalry*. New York: Norton, 1987.

Authors of *Liberated Children/Liberated Parents* now address this common problem. Explores background of this issue and suggests ways to prevent and ameliorate sibling rivalry.

Franke, Linda Bird. *Growing Up Divorced*. New York: Linden Press, 1983.

This book is the outgrowth of an article that was originally a cover story in *Newsweek*. It is based on the eloquent responses of children, reflecting on their feelings about their parents' divorces. Offers advice to parents in helping children cope according to their developmental level. Franke discusses the special problems of children 6-8 (The Age of Sadness) and 9-12 (The Age of Anger). *Growing Up Divorced* is one of the better books available on this topic.

Fuchs, Lawrence H. *Family Matters: Why the American Family Is in Trouble*. New York: Random House, 1972.

Attributes the tension in American families to the conflict between a commitment to the ideals of independence and equality and the conditions of dependency and inequality that mark our family and society. Closely examines the family system of today, pointing out sources of conflict at each stage of development.

Gerson, Kathleen. *Hard Choices*. Berkeley: University of California Press, 1985.

Results of a study involving interviews with 63 women between 27 and 37 years of age concerning their choices of career, working, marriage, number of children, and income.

Greywolf, Elizabeth S. *The Single Mother's Handbook: The Practical Guide for Coping with Children, Money, Time, and Work*. New York: Quill, 1984.

This book grew out of a research project at the Stress and Family Project at Harvard. It addresses the demanding role of the single parent. Chapter topics include, "Time Management: Making

Every Minute Count," "What If I Need Welfare?", and "Sex and Love in Your New Life."

Grollman, Earl A., and Gerri L. Sweder. *The Working Parent Dilemma: How to Balance the Responsibility of Children and Careers.* Boston: Beacon Press, 1986.

Recognizing that the definition of childhood and family are changing, the authors asked over 1,000 school children how they got along with their parents--what they appreciated, and what they were unhappy about. Based on those answers, Grollman and Sweder suggest ways for parents to become more involved in the everyday lives of their children and how to reduce strains in family relations. A bibliography for each topic is included.

Howard, Jane. *Families.* New York: Simon and Schuster, 1978.

This book is a tribute to the qualities of endurance of the modern family, in spite of all the changes it has undergone, and the rumors of its demise. The author visits a variety of families across the country and examines their kinship network.

Kalter, Suzy. *Instant Parent: A Guide for Stepparents, Part-Time Parents and Grandparents.* New York: A & W Publishers, 1979.

An amusing book about the pitfalls of caring for "inherited" children. Contains advice and specific information on a wide range of situations, such as, "How to gain a child's respect--without bribery." Contains a 30 day calendar of places to go, things to do, projects to participate in, and things to make with children of all ages.

Levitan, Sar A., and Richard S. Bellows. *What's Happening to the American Family?* Baltimore: Johns Hopkins University Press, 1981.

The report of a study, funded by the Ford Foundation, by the George Washington University Center for Social Policy Studies. Their findings indicate that although there have been radical shifts from traditional patterns, the family remains a resilient institution. Includes an overview of government social policies directed at families.

Lundberg, Ferdinand. *The Coming World Transformation.* Garden City, N.Y.: Doubleday, 1963.

A provocative, rather negative appraisal of the future status of family life as we know it. Author believes that the family is near the point of complete extinction, except for the early years of child rearing.

Lynn, David B. *The Father: His Role in Child Development.* Monterey, Calif.: Brooks/Cole, 1974.

Examines the role of the father from a cultural perspective and the nuances of father-child relationships. The author, a developmental psychologist at the University of California, Davis, has drawn material from research, history, literature, and anthropology.

Norris, Gloria, and Jo Ann Miller. *The Working Mothers' Complete Handbook*. Revised ed. New York: New American Library, 1984.

Helpful hints for the busy and conscientious working mother. Practical, first-hand information on just about every subject in a well-organized book. Child development and parenting advice that is based on sound principles.

Parke, Ross D. *Fathers*. Cambridge: Harvard University Press , 1981.

A complete and readable guide to psychology's new understanding of the relationship between father and child. Relates how an involved and caring father can make a difference in the life of his child and the whole family. Covers such topics as intellectual development, divorce and custody, and innovations in fathering. Includes an annotated list of suggested readings. A volume in the *Developing Child Series*.

Radl, Shirley L. *How To Be a Mother and a Person Too*. New York: Rawson Wade, 1979.

A humorous, yet practical, look at child-centeredness, which tends to ignore a mother's feelings and emotional needs. Examples of chapter titles are, "How Sticking it to Mother Became a National Pastime (and How to Fight Back)," "The Complete Guide to Maternal Guilt," and "How to Escape the What-Will People-Think Trap."

Rogers, Fred. *Mister Rogers Talks with Families about Divorce*. New York: Berkley, 1987.

Another "how to" book for helping children of all ages through the painful process of divorce. Includes advice on everything from how to break the news to coping with holidays.

Rosin, Mark Bruce. *Stepfathering: A Stepfather's Advice on Creating a New Family*. New York: Simon and Schuster, 1987.

Discusses the many aspects of stepparenting that differ from biological parenting. This book is based on interviews with 50 stepfathers, asking what they thought and how they felt about their roles. The consensus opinion is that there is "no right way to do it," and that there is a continual process of adjusting and readjusting that stepfathers, spouses, stepchildren, and biological children go through.

Sanger, Sirgay, and John Kelly. *The Woman Who Works, The Parent Who Cares: A Revolutionary Program for Raising Your Child.* Boston: Little, Brown, 1987.

Optimistically assesses the influence of a woman's work on the psychological development of her children. Contains practical advice on maintaining discipline from afar for parents of infants and older children as well. Discusses the need for the working parent to set priorities which meet her needs as well as those of her children.

Schwam, Jeffrey S., and Maria Krocker Tuskan. "The Adopted Child." *Basic Handbook of Child Psychiatry.* Joseph P. Noshpitz, Editor-in--Chief. Volume 1. New York: Basic Books, 1979, pp. 342-348.

Consolidates clinical experiences and research on adoption with emphasis on characteristics and reactions of adopted children and adoptive parents. Includes extensive bibliography.

Takas, Marianne. *Child Custody: A Complete Guide for Concerned Mothers.* New York: Harper and Row, 1987.

A very useful book for any mother facing litigation in a child custody case. Written by a Boston attorney, *Child Custody* provides information on where to find help, what laws are applicable, and how to pursue a child custody case. The appendix contains recommended readings and legal advocacy resources.

PLAY DURING MIDDLE CHILDHOOD

Almost two decades ago, the London Institute of Contemporary Arts and the Welsh Arts Consul sponsored a contest. Entrants were asked to design an object of play or a toy, defining the symbolic meaning of toy and play. Participants were creative people challenged by the idea of the contest. They were not psychologists, child development experts, teachers, toy manufacturers, or marketers. Their answers were insightful, wise, and creative. Here are a few.

Play seems to be both disinterested and passionate at the same time; disinterested in that it is not for real, and passionate in the absorption it requires....A good toy must balance the toymaker's inventiveness against the player's inventiveness. If a toy is too well-defined by its maker, it becomes inflexible to play with and consequently boring. If, on the other hand, it is too loosely defined, it will fail to provide the stimulus necessary to make it worth playing with.--Oliver Bevan.

Toys are part of playing. Playing involves the creative or fanciful participation in isolated real life processes or skills without regard to scale, time, place, or consequence.--Kenneth Armitage

A toy is a highly translatable object requiring participation.--Michael Punt.[1]

Children at the elementary school age are still actively involved in play and toys. The content, variety of play, the manipulative skills necessary for play, and the perseverance in play, all reach a high during middle childhood. Play can take on many forms that change as the child changes and grows. The ever increasing complex nature of child's play reflects the child's newly acquired skills and abilities. Increased cognitive competence during the elementary school years results in the increased complexity of play.

Play in which the goal is to manipulate objects to create is known as constructive play. As a child enters middle childhood a good amount of activity is constructive. This includes such pleasur-

---

[1]Frank and Theresa Caplan, *The Power of Play*. (New York: Anchor, 1974), 309-312.

able pastimes as art projects and puzzles. Children become absorbed in these self-initiated, nonconflictive activities. By participating in this play learning they discover from and form relationships. They coordinate seeing and moving. The amount of flexibility and creativity allowed in play is determined by the amount of flexibility and creativity of the play materials set out. Highly structured materials such as puzzles are devoid of inventive and divergent play compared to play produced by less structured art and building materials. Unstructured creative play produces unusual and imaginative variations of old activities and skills.

Object play encourages not only creativity but intellectual curiosity as well. As a child observes the multiplicity of an object, he or she must put these into the context of life and create an image. The more experienced and mature the child, the broader the applicability the object obtains. Children enjoy mastering objects and understanding their unique characteristics.

It is possible that children spend so much time in structured play because schools focus on constructive activities. If that is so, the setting, which is frequently the school, determines the play behavior. Developmentally appropriate constructive play activities help children to view school as challenging, meaningful, and pleasurable.

Dramatic or imaginary play peaks during the kindergarten and first-grade years, then begins to decline as the child becomes increasingly more social. The child must be able to separate the literal meaning of a situation and generalize it to an imaginary situation for dramatic play to occur. Play, therefore, becomes an internal process with recognition of logical and abstract thoughts, as well as physical processes. The child has to experience what he or she thinks the situation is supposed to be before the situation can be manipulated to create a new experience or absurdity. This is an aspect of early middle childhood humor. Putting a coat on backwards can be humorous to a first grader only because the first grader knows that a coat is not made to be worn backwards.

Dramatic play also allows children to play the game of life. Real life situations can be acted out, changed, and redirected without ever having to be actually experienced. This promotes the ability to find meaning behind others' behavior. From around six to eight years of age children realize that others can have a perspective different or similar to theirs. However, children are not yet able to coordinate their viewpoints. A one-dimensional perspective exists.

From eight to 10 years of age the child begins to form a coordinated chain of perspectives. The child is aware and influenced by others' viewpoints. Role playing allows a child to reflectively put one's self in another's place and act out and judge the other's intentions.

By the end of middle childhood, around 10 to 12 years of age, the child can mentally role play the mutual actions and intentions of self and others and reflect from a third person perspective. Pretend play is emotionally satisfying to young children. The relationship of the relatively powerless child versus the powerful adult in the real world can be reversed in play. Children can put themselves in control and imitate the authority figures in their lives. They can role play adult functions and experiences.

Expression of forbidden or embarrassing emotions can be released through dramatic play. Being scared or angry can be experienced through a pretend situation. A child can yell at a doll and release tension and anger without fear of reprisal. The roles children play become more complex as they mature.

Children should not be discouraged from imaginary or pretend play. Imaginative play alone can be active or take the form of daydreaming. During this time it is necessary for children to sort out experiences and reflect, to think about how they would change a situation and explore their hopes and dreams. These moments should be welcomed by parents for they are thought to be the foundations of creativity.

As children become proficient at reading, they will gradually cease to daydream out loud but may pursue a road to fantasy through books. This provides a healthy release from the stress of daily life. Knowing how to enjoy being alone starts with enjoyment of early dramatic play alone.

Game play increases from kindergarten through the fourth or fifth grade and thereafter begins a gradual decline reaching a low in the early teen years. Game play necessitates a child's recognition and acceptance of conformity to rules imposed on a pleasurable activity. In games, unlike any other form of play, there can be no modifications allowed unless all players agree before the game begins. The rules dictate the roles of the players. Play is goal oriented. Each player plays to win. Cooperation, competition, and challenge exist. Children need the physical and mental skills required by the game to enjoy the challenge. Games that are too easy or too hard bore or frustrate the child. Challenging competition implies vying for recognition, and feelings of envy may surface. Success reinforces a child's self-esteem. Game play runs the gamut from board games like "Candyland" or "Monopoly" to organized sports such as touch football.

Some children feel uncomfortable in organized group games. They need to watch first to feel safe in trying later. These children should never be forced into an embarrassing situation. Invite them again to try after having watched from the sidelines. They will enter the game when they feel comfortable.

Early elementary school-age children have rigid views of right and wrong. They are apt to lose their temper easily if they feel another player has acted unfairly. Parents cannot fight their children's battles but they can listen sympathetically and clarify what has occurred. Role settling by children is a slow development nurtured by maturity and experience.

Most children have come to the realization by middle childhood that sharing and cooperation are necessary social skills. For many, however, a mixed message is being sent. That message is an emphasis on "winning." This is frequently apparent in children's organized sports programs. A program that over-emphasizes winning can lead to psychological problems for many children. Nonathletic children may experience such reproach and sense of failure that they will turn away from athletics forever. Overambitious coaches choose players to win, not for equal participation. The child who is constantly passed over and criticized may be made to feel of little self-worth.

Sports nonachievers are only half of the problem. Ronald Smith and Frank Smoll, authors of *Kids Sports: A Survival Guide for Parents*[2] suggests that there is another side of the coin: the pressured elite athlete.

Organized sports need not pose potential problems to children if the goals of the program recognize the need for fun and stimulation of interpersonal growth. Team sports can provide an early lesson in interdependence. Subordination of one's own goals to those that are best for the team and a division of labor to realize these goals, are important in training for later adult life. Team inclusion suggests a responsibility that one's actions can affect the success or failure of all. Team success shines on even the least skilled player and team failure can caste a shadow on even the best player.

Team play which stresses prosocial attitudes can help the child to conceptualize an overall plan and anticipate the consequences of their actions on the group at large. It is important for parents to remember that children cannot always recognize misguided leadership of team sports. Parents should be aware of not just the final score but how the game is played and, if necessary, apply pressure to coaches who value points more than sensitive kids' feelings.

The stimulus of good play is a good imagination and good toys. The basic criteria for evaluating the quality of a toy are as follows:

1. Is the toy free of excess detail?
2. Does the toy allow for versatility in use?
3. Does the toy actively involve the child in the play?
4. Is the toy manipulative enough for the child to use easily?
5. Is the material the toy is made of comfortable and pleasant to the touch?
6. Is the construction and use of the toy easily understood?
7. Is the toy durable?
8. Does the toy work as described on the package or advertisement?
9. If the toy comes with component parts, has the manufacturer included an adequate quantity?

---

[2](New York: Addison-Wesley, 1983).

10. If the toy is meant to hold the child, is it sturdy enough and does it allow for ample space per child?
11. If the toy is intended to be used in play with more than one child, does it encourage cooperative play?
12. Is the price of the toy reasonable in relationship to its durability, play value, and amount of use?

Purchasers of toys should be reminded that not all toys marketed promote positive growth in children. Parents must be discriminating in their purchases. A quick walk through any toy department reveals the heavy promotion of war and war-like toys which are estimated to have increased in sales greatly over the past three years, according to the National Coalition on Television Violence. In a Fall 1985 press release, this group reported that seven of the leading 10 toys in the country were violent and that the average American child viewed 800 television advertisements a year promoting war toys. Selling war toys, games, and guns to children is a big and profitable business. United States sales were projected at over a billion dollars in 1985 alone.

Why shouldn't children play with war toys, war games, and guns? Haven't toy guns been marketed to children for generations? Noted researcher on violent toys, Charles W. Turner of the University of Utah suggests that playing with violent toys increases the risk that children will use aggression in real life behavior.[3]

Playing with violent toys that elicit aggressive behavior hardens children to the dangers and potential harm of violent behavior. The more desensitized children become, the increased risk that they will resort to violent behavior in real life.

Parents should educate their children about the dangers of violent entertainment. They should explain that massive advertising campaigns don't necessarily mean good toys but are the manufacturers' desires to sell toys and maximize profits. Additionally, parents should restrict their purchases to toys that promote prosocial behavior.

Wisely selected toys should enrich the child's play and skills. They should teach and bring enjoyment. Toys should stimulate sensory and creative experiences as well as work towards energy release.

Play can also be influenced by the environment in which it occurs. The shape, size, and contour of the play area can determine the nature of the play. Playground construction influences use of the available equipment. Creative playgrounds with mobile equipment that can change configurations and suggest many uses will produce more imaginative play. Traditional playgrounds with conventional equip-

---

[3]Charles Turner, "Effects of Toy Guns and Airplanes on Children's Antisocial Freeplay Behavior," *Journal of Experimental Child Psychology* (1976): 303-315.

ment such as swings and seesaws produces traditional structured, functional play. Structured playground play can lead to boredom. When children feel bored they will attempt dangerous variations of the play equipment. Walking up slides rather than sliding down and swinging from the knees can prove to be a precarious challenge. New approaches to playground planning incorporate creative, bold structures that stimulate the child's imagination and encourage social and physical action. Play equipment and materials should not overpower or thwart the child. They should be in proper scale to the child's size. Aesthetically pleasing tunnels and caves, tree climbers, wavy walls, and animal sculptures encourage children to run, jump, climb, hide, explore, and pretend.

Well-planned play areas where boys and girls can engage in rough and tumble activities such as tag and catch, can reduce the incidence of playground injury and accident. In *Children: Development through Adolescence*, Allison Clarke-Stewart and Joanne Barbara Koch note the historical change in activity preference between boys and girls.[4] They suggest that middle childhood girls are more like boys in their game and activity choices today than at the turn of the century. They choose active sports such as baseball that were once the province of boys. Boys have taken up more vigorous and macho games such as football and wrestling."

Studies have found that girls can play with so-called "boys'" toys with little criticism from their peers, but boys on the other hand are scorned by their peers if they play with "girls'" toys. Changes in children's activity choices reflect changes in our culture at large.

Play is essential for a child's development. It encourages intellectual stimulation and language development. Emotional and social growth are furthered. Physical growth and coordination are strengthened, and creative and independent behavior are enhanced. Children's play is critical in promoting overall development. Through play children learn the rules, roles and values of society. As Jerome Brunner has stated "play is the principal business of childhood.[5]

---

[4](New York: Wiley, 1983), p. 351.

[5]Jerome Brunner, "Play Is Serious Business," Psychology Today, 8 (1975): 80-83.

BIBLIOGRAPHY

Adcock, Don. *Your Child at Play*. New York: Newmarket Press, 1985.

Discusses the role of development and its relationship to play. The text stresses the importance of children's exploration of the environment and what they learn through play.

Anderson, Valerie, and Carl Bereiter. *Thinking Games*. Belmont, Calif.: Pitman Learning, 1980.

Designed to illustrate how children experience enjoyment while exercising thinking abilities. No special materials are required. The games emphasize competition between teams rather than individuals. Planned primarily for teachers, this book can be equally useful with other groups of children in the five-to-nine age range. The activities aid in development of language, math, strategy, nonverbal communication, perceptual organization, and rhythmic skills.

Attebury, Jean E. *Project Plans to Build for Children from the Pages of Better Homes and Gardens*. Des Moines, Ia.: Garlinhouse, 1984.

Instructions and diagrams are given for building over 130 projects from toys to room design. Order forms are included for instructions for additional projects.

Axline, Virginia. *Playtherapy*. New York: Ballantine, 1974.

Playtherapy is a technique where children express their feelings of hatred, loneliness, and inadequacy through play in an effort to learn about, accept, and respect themselves. *Playtherapy* is authoritative and well written. A classic in its field.

Baker, Bruce. *Play Skills*. Champaign, Ill.: Research Press, 1984.

Combines play, learning, and fun. This manual provides a step-by-step approach to teaching play skills to special needs children. Teaching methods are illustrated through specific examples. A checklist to measure the child's current skill level is given. Suggested reading for parents and teachers of special needs children.

Beckwith, Glenwood J. *How to Make Your Backyard More Interesting Than T.V.* New York: McGraw-Hill, 1980.

Offers helpful guidelines for creating developmentally appropriate play environments. Safety of play equipment is stressed.

Bettelheim, Bruno. *The Uses of Enchantment: The Meaning and Importance of Fairy Tales*. New York: Random, 1977.

World-renowned child psychologist evaluates the irreplaceable value of fairy tales for children. Stressed is the use of and need for fairy tales to help the child master the psychological problems of growing up. *The Uses of Enchantment* is fascinating reading for anyone interested in children.

Bond, Tim. *Games for Social and Life Skills*. New York: Nichols, 1985.

The author utilizes social interactions within groups, through games as a means of social education. Seventy-eight games with worksheets and questionnaires are included. Games have been selected on the basis of their usefulness with young people. Recommended for teachers to use in the classroom.

Bottomly, Jim. *Paper Projects for Creative Kids of All Ages*. Boston: Little, 1983.

This is a well-illustrated book chock full of fun paper projects. Techniques are simple and materials used are low cost.

Bronfenbrenner, Urie. *Two Worlds of Childhood: U.S. and U.S.S.R.* New York: Russell Sage Foundation, 1970.

Compares child-rearing practices of the world's two strongest powers. There are descriptions of children's play in each society. How play activity is used by each society in terms of its effects on the moral, ethical, and social development is discussed. Play is not the specific focus of the study. It is considered one of the many childhood activities that contribute to the development of personality and character. The significance of these activities, including television viewing, is examined in terms of the kind of citizen these activities tend to foster.

Brown, Catherine Caldwell, and Allen W. Gottfried. *Play Interactions: The Role of Toys and Parental Involvement in Children's Development*. Pediatric Round Table #11. Somerville, N.J.: Johnson & Johnson, 1985.

Explores the research findings of 20 child development authorities concerning the origin of play, play and developmental processes, the social significance of play, and consequences of play. Evidence is presented that shows play materials and parental involvement as potent factors related to the development of young children.

Caballero, Jane. *Art Projects for Young Children*. Atlanta: Humanics, 1981.

Contains over 100 projects in the areas of drawing, painting,

puppetry, clay, printing, photography and more. This book is a resource for primary school teachers and parents who want to encourage their child's creative growth at home.

Ellington, Henry. *A Handbook of Game Design*. New York: Nichols,
1982.

Tips and tricks on game board design are given. Teachers can
make their own games around classroom curriculum with the help of
this volume. A guide for making games challenging and fun.

Ellington, Henry. *Case Studies in Game Design*. New York: Nichols,
1984.

An in-depth examination of all types of games ranging from
board games to computer games. The authors look at the strategies
behind the design as well as the tactical thinking necessary for play.
Helpful to teachers designing their own game materials.

Friedberg, M. Paul. *Playgrounds for City Children*. Wheaton, Md.:
Association for Childhood Education International, 1982.

Promotes the idea that children's learning can be increased by
improving children's play environments. Imaginative presentations for
playgrounds are included by the author who is a landscape architect.
This low cost, short book should be read if a restructured or new
play area is being considered.

Frost, Joe. *Children's Play and Playgrounds*. Rockleigh, N.J.: Longwood, 1981.

Offers essays, photos, drawings, and playground plans. Ideas are
given for improving or designing children's playspace. A special section on playgrounds for handicapped children is included. An excellent resource for PTA's and other groups establishing playgrounds.

Garvey, Catherine. *Play*. Cambridge, Mass.: Harvard University
Press, 1977.

Attempts to provide answers to the question, "What is Play?"
Defines the types and boundaries of play while acknowledging both
its similarities to and differences from real life. The book begins at
infancy, with a main focus on the first five years of life. However,
there is a framework established that applies to later years. A volume in the *Developing Child Series*. Ideal for parents and students.

Headley, Keith E., et al. *Play: Children's Business*. Washington, D.C.:
Association for Childhood Education International, 1979.

These essays illustrate the relationship of play to cognition, to
development, and to socialization. Practical suggestions are offered

for implementing good play experiences and selecting materials that provide children not only with opportunities for play but comfortable play changes. There is a guide to play materials and age-appropriate toys.

Hodgson, Harriet. *"I Made It Myself": Creative Toys Kids Can Make from Stuff around the House*. New York: Warner, 1986.

An easy-to-read and use book for creative play. Illustrations are provided. Written for parents to use with young children.

Johnson, June. *838 Ways to Amuse a Child*. New York: Harper & Row, 1983.

This paperback volume is a storehouse of imaginative activities for children. Craft, hobby projects, science experiments, nature studies, and games are listed. Additional resources for materials and information are included.

Kamii, Constance, and Rheta DeVries. *Group Games in Early Education: Implications of Piaget's Theory*. Washington, D.C.: National Association for the Education of Young Children, 1980.

How do games contribute to children's development? Why use them? What are some good ones? What effect does competition have on the child? These questions and more are answered from a Piagetian viewpoint.

Levick, Myra. *Mommy, Daddy, Look What I'm Saying*. New York: Evans, 1985.

Simplified guidelines provide a means of understanding children's needs. Helps parents find meaning in children's behavior in relation to nonverbal expression. Benchmarks for growth are illustrated through artwork. Common warning signals are included.

Linderman, Emma. *Teachables from Trashables: Homemade Toys That Teach*. St. Paul: Toys'n Things Press, 1979.

Illustrates how to turn common household items into educational toys. Instructions are shown for each toy. A fun resource for parents and teachers of young children.

Liss, Marsha. *Social and Cognitive Skills, Sex Roles and Children's Play*. Orlando: Academic Press, 1983.

Explores how sex role affects a child's development. Children's play is viewed from cognitive, behavioral, social learning, and original theoretical perspectives. For educators and child development professionals.

Marzollo, Jean. *Superkids*. New York: Harper & Row, 1982.

Provides learning and play activities for children from kindergarten through the elementary grades and up. Creativity is stressed. This is a resource for children as well as a guide for parents and teachers looking for activity ideas.

Mergen, B. *Play and Playthings: A Reference Guide*. Westport, Conn.: Greenwood, 1982.

Mergen presents an historical reference guide to children's play in America. Writings on children and child behavior are studies in an effort to understand what is meant by the word "play" and what play has meant to children. Pictures of children playing in different parts of the country, in different time periods, are included.

Milberg, A. *Street Games*. New York: McGraw-Hill, 1976.

Instructions for games of interest to school-age children are given in this volume. The historical origin of each game is discussed. An informative book for anyone interested in children's play.

Moore, Gary T. *Bibliography on Children and the Built Environment: Child Care Centers, Outdoor Play Environments, and Other Children's Environments*. Milwaukee: University of Wisconsin Center for Architecture and Urban Planning Research, 1979.

A bibliography created for use by U.S. military installations. Practical information. Useful for individuals developing child care centers.

Newson, John, and Elizabeth Newson. *Toys and Playthings*. New York: Pantheon Books, 1979.

The Newson's take a look at toys in connection with the growing child. Concern is not for the right toy for the right age but rather what toy is appropriate for a particular stage of the child's development. Describes the many fascinations kids have with toys.

Oppenheim, JoAnne. *Kids and Play*. New York: Ballantine, 1984.

Shows parents how to get the most learning out of play without taking the fun away. This is an educationally-based handbook that offers supportive advice for parents.

Pepler, D.J., and K.H. Robin. *The Play of Children*. New York: Karger, 1982.

This scholarly volume is of interest to educators, researchers, and those persons with background knowledge of the area. *The Play of Children* is divided into five parts covering interest areas such as ecological influences on children's play. Contributions to each section are made by well-known experts.

Piers, Maria W., and Genevieve M. Landau. *The Gift of Play: And Why Young Children Cannot Thrive without It.* New York: Walker, 1980.

Piers and Landau regard imagination and free play as more beneficial to the child's development than structured, goal-oriented play activity. The premise of this book is that play is a rehearsal for adulthood and provides a transition to it. The authors suggest that activities such as television deprive a child of the imaginative and active play required for this transition. Educators and teachers alike will find this interesting reading.

Robinson, Jeri. *Activities for Anyone, Anytime, Anywhere.* Boston: Little, Brown, 1983.

Designed for children and adults, Robinson's creative, imaginative book is filled with ideas for activities for any place and any kind of situation. This is a good book to keep around the house or classroom.

Rogovin, Anne. *Let Me Do It!* New York: Crowell, 1980.

Includes projects suitable for both the exceptional and the normal child. Activities include puppet making. Ideas using bottles, boxes, plants, and animals to teach concepts are given. Suggestions incorporate nursery rhymes, fables, and stories. The activities are simple with clear directions.

Schaefer, Charles, and Kevin O'Connor. *Handbook of Play Therapy.* New York, Wiley, 1983.

Integrates the theoretical and practical with recent developments in the field of play therapy. This book is distinguished in that it shows how to modify theoretical orientations to meet the needs of different populations and individuals. Clinicians will find this useful.

Schaefer, Charles, and Steven Reid. *Game Play, Therapeutic Use of Childhood Games.* New York: Wiley, 1986.

An interesting book on the therapeutic value of games. Topics covered include the use of games to improve social skills, communications, and the ability to cope with competition. A unique theoretical, yet practical resource.

Schwartzman, Helen B., ed. *Play and Culture.* West Point, N.Y.: Leisure Press, 1980.

Play theory, the ritual dimensions of play, linguistic play, children's play, game play, and the playful aspects of humor are considered. Theoretical orientation for professionals.

Shapiro, Lawrence E. *Games to Grow On: Activities to Help Children Learn Self-Control*. Englewood Cliffs, N.J.: Prentice-Hall, 1981.

Understanding the value of play during the child's growing years and the role of play at different developmental stages is the focus of this book. Practical ideas to stimulate play are suggested. This book can provide parents and teachers with a fresh appreciation of the area.

Singer, Dorothy, and Jerome Singer. *Partners in Play: A Step-by-Step Guide to Imaginative Play in Children*. New York: Harper & Row, 1977.

The Singer's are a distinguished husband and wife team of educators. In this book they establish a theoretical framework for imaginative play and provide specific activities designed to enhance children's imaginative play experiences. There are helpful chapters on play materials, indoor/outdoor play environments, activities for children on trips, and home toy construction instructions.

Sobel, Jeff. *Everybody Wins*. New York: Walker, 1982.

This book is a collection of noncompetitive games for use with children up to 10 years of age. Included are word games, games of imagination, and active and passive games. Sharing and cooperation are stressed.

Sponseller, Doris, ed. *Play as a Learning Medium*. Washington, D.C.: National Association for the Education of Young Children, 1974.

Concentrates on the cognitive developmental role of play. The contributors, all of whom are well-known educators, focus on the role of play in the child's total development. Though this is an older publication of The National Association for the Education of Young Children, it is still valuable reading.

Sternlicht, Manny, and Abraham Hurwitz. *Games Children Play: Instructive and Creative Play Activities for the Mentally Retarded and Developmentally Disabled Child*. New York: Van Nostrand Reinhold, 1981.

Intended for parents and teachers, this book provides play activities designed to stimulate the psychological growth of learning-disabled children. In order to help the parent or professional place the various games in proper perspective, the psychological principles underlying play behavior are given as well as the chronological stages of play development. Included is a helpful section of suggested reading.

Strom, Robert. *Growing through Play: Readings for Parents and Teachers*. Monterey, Calif.: Brooks-Cole, 1980.

A comprehensive collection about play by different experts in the area of child development. Areas of discussion include the growth promoted by play, observation of play, the role of solitary play, and suggestions for playground planning. Through this book parents and teachers can gain a basic understanding of this important area in the life of children.

Sutton-Smith, Brian. *Toys as Play Culture*. New York: Gardner Press, 1986.

Examines the role of toys in contemporary society. The premise that toys are more than playthings is presented. Toys as objects of attachment and companionship are examined in the author's theory.

U.S. Department of Health and Human Services, Public Health Service. *Caring about Kids: The Importance of Play*. Publication No. 81-969. Rockville, Md.: National Institute of Mental health, 1981.

Children's play is a developmental imperative. Just as crucial is how teachers and parents understand and react to children and their play. Play is a child's rehearsal for life. Book provides opportunities to try and test all kinds of roles and situations. This short but important publication is available free of charge and makes valuable reading for parents and teachers.

Weinstein, Matt. *Playfair: Everybody's Guide to Non-Competitive Play*. San Luis Obispo, Calif.: Impact, 1980.

Stresses that everyone can win and will win in noncompetitive play. The games offered are flexible enough for use from childhood through the senior years. Ideas on how to invent your own games are given.

Westland, Cor, and Jane Knight. *Playing, Living, Learning: A World-wide Perspective on Children's Opportunities to Play*. State College, Pa.: Ventura, 1982.

Detailed and comprehensive study on the various forms and patterns of children's play around the world. Designed to motivate and inspire all who are interested in children. It serves as a valuable resource in the worldwide struggle for the recognition of the value of play. Included is a guide to international and national organizations relevant to the subject of play.

Winnicott, Donald. *Playing and Reality*. New York: Basic Books, 1971.

Winnicott, a well-known psychoanalytic therapist, links play with creativity and developmental levels. An esoteric approach presents play as a healthy, natural activity. Written for the professional practitioner.

Yawkey, Thomas. *Child's Play: Developmental and Applied.* Hillsdale, N.J.: Erlbaum, 1984.

Examines the origins and nature of symbolic play. The contribution that play makes to cognitive and social development is discussed. This volume provides theoretical coverage of the art of child's play and is best utilized by the child development professional.

PEER RELATIONSHIPS DURING MIDDLE CHILDHOOD

As children gradually establish more ties to the world outside their home, their peer group takes on a larger degree of importance. Friendships for children provide a source of great pleasure as well as disillusionment and frustration. As elementary school-age children move into the world of their peers, recognizing the same faces of friends and acquaintances each day is reassuring. Friends can affect a child's pattern of socialization. What they play, wear, and think takes on importance. Friendships are a central ingredient in the lives of elementary school-age children.

To be accepted by one's peers, children must learn to cope and control their own behavior. They must learn to give and take. While they master the social rules and morality of their peers, they develop and refine their own social skills. Social skills are defined as techniques for initiating and sustaining interpersonal relationships and interactions.

During the middle childhood years, as children gradually widen their experiences and cognitively grow, they are able to accurately understand the thoughts and emotions of others. They are able to project their own feelings into an event, and realize and understand another person's feelings, emotions, needs, and suffering. Empathy is established.

This ability to be sensitive to others is associated with helpfulness. But this alone may not be enough in our culture to produce a child who will act to help another. The development of pro-social behavior is influenced by the competitive society we live in. Cooperative and competitive behavior co-exist. As competitiveness increases with age, children are not as willing to show compassion. This is particularly true for boys who are most likely to receive praise for competitiveness. Girls are more frequently rewarded for showing helpful, cooperative behavior.

Using social skills to make new friends can often be a difficult task. By middle childhood, children have already developed a desire for the company of same-sex peers. Cliques and clubs of friends become commonplace. Penetrating the invisible barriers of these groups can be a formidable undertaking for children with even the best of social skills.

Child development research points to distinct functions of children's friendships. They provide children with the opportunity to learn and practice social skills, and promote companionship between same and similar age peers. Friendships allow children to compare themselves physically, intellectually,and socially with other children. This comparison is not competitive but evaluative for the child. Friendships also foster a feeling of group belonging. Children acquire emotional security from a single close relationship with a parent or caretaker. They obtain a feeling of community from interactions with neighbors and friends. Early friendships have consequences that last and have an impact on each phase of a child's development.

Some children are able to attract friends more easily than others.[1] What are some of the characteristics that draw friends to a particular child? Physical attractiveness is important in children's selection of friends. Studies have shown that children ascribe more positive qualities to good-looking children.

Popular children with moderate levels of aspiration are also more likely to be academic achievers. Children perceived to be over or underachievers are less favored, as are those children with unusual names. Names affect a child's acceptance. Children in middle childhood perceive common names as the most attractive.

Popular children are quick to lavish praise on their peers and accept such from others. They are adaptable and conform to the needs of the situation. Less popular children are perceived to be more show-offish, babyish, aggressive, and less resourceful.

Different patterns of friendship characterize boys and girls in this age group. Boys tend to huddle in large groups of buddies. Girls tend to consider the group to be a twosome of close friends. These different patterns of friendship are rooted in early childhood play experiences. Boys and girls engage in different sports and games. While girls enjoy jumping rope with a single close friend, boys enjoy baseball and football. Such sports require mutual cooperation and joint collaboration of skills. Within these larger groups boys are taught social skills applicable and pertinent to a contemporary organizational structure of life. Boys learn to work in harmony and get along with other boys whom they might or might not especially like. Learning such skills can be useful to a boy, or a girl, in future years. Inclusion in this large group supports a boy's pursuit for autonomy. It provides boys with the sense of collective participation in an atmosphere of group solidarity.

Though girls today have become much more like boys in their game play and activity choices, they do not seem to require the same solidarity of group support. Girls view the bonds of friendships as a network of emotional intimacy. They more often play in pairs in contrast to boys' playing in groups. For girls, the old adage of "two's company, three's a crowd" seems to hold true. Girls view friends as significant sources of support and confidence. This view

---

[1]R.M. Lerner, "Effects of Age, Sex, and Physical Attractiveness on Child-Peer Relations, Academic Performance, and Elementary School Adjustment." *Developmental Psychology* 45(1974): 305-310.

nurtures the emotional aptitudes relevant for close interpersonal relationships and maternal behaviors necessary in later years.

Regardless of the child's sex, these close relationships bring both positive and negative consequences. It is most positive for children to develop the skills necessary to make friends. It is advantageous for children to be adroit at maintaining these friendships. However, negative consequences include learning to spurn others and cast aside friendships. Close friendships in the middle childhood years can be fragile. The same close, and sometimes demanding, friendships that provide trust and encouragement, can give rise to anger, indignation, suspicion, and jealousy. Through these interpersonal problems of the elementary school years, children learn the social meanings of inclusion, exclusion, conformity, and independence.

Child development research points to three specific ways group membership can be established. An individual child with sophisticated social skills, leadership, and talent can be a focal point of the group's structure. Other children, attracted to the leader's dynamic personality characteristics, become secondary in this group. They gain acceptance by gaining the leader's approval.

The second method of group construction begins with an ongoing friendship or tie between two peers. As these children include other peers in their activities, the group grows. The so-called child-initiated "official clubs" of middle childhood are examples of this method. In the formation and dissolution of these clubs, children are experimenting in the structure of social organization. They develop an understanding of groups; from conception as a disorganized group of people, to a view of groups as an organized collective. They experience a sense of deep participation within the framework of organizational rules, and an environment of mutual support and assistance.

The last method of group formation is based principally on group participation in a common interest or activity. Children involved in team sports are prime examples of this type of group formation. An essential requirement in this group is the necessary skill and interest to take part.

These methods of group formation breed comparatively homogeneous associations. Children select friends with similar interests and skills. In other words, children pick friends who are like themselves. In all of these formations, the group becomes the social entity which produces resources and support. The significance of this mutual aid system increases as the child gradually leaves the safety of the home and family for the world of peers.

Having considered the importance of the peer group, one must question what happens to a child when there is a disruption in this process. During middle childhood the child is mastering the art of belonging, desiring active interplay with friends and acquaintances. Social pressures are existent. Aggressive behavior, secretiveness, and fluctuations of moods are common hallmarks of this age. They signify the child's attempts at independence.

Disruptions such as losing a friend is a stress-producing hardship. It creates a crisis which temporarily burdens a child's normal coping process. Developmental characteristics may be intensified and magnified. Children may react with a sense of grief to the loss of a close friend. Surrendering the companionship, camaraderie, and support of a trusted peer can leave the child feeling alone. Loneliness, depression, and anger may be a temporary expression in response to the child's despair.

If the change is due to extreme circumstances that force a child to change the daily environment, such as the school, there may be greater disruption. Anticipation of integrating into a new social milieu, where everyone appears to have known each other for a long time, can cause further distress. Anxiety can accompany this distress. In severe situations, such anxiety can renew all the traumas and problems of starting school for the first time, or other moves that necessitated a school change.

Severe anxiety can restrict the child's problem-solving abilities. The child's resources to produce novel and accommodating solutions to his problems may be limited. Defensive or maladaptive reactions may be in response to the anxiety that accompanies the situation. Rejection, abandonment, and/or feelings of lack of love can make the elementary school-age child act out. Aggression in children of this age is viewed negatively by peers and teachers.

Anxiety and the forced dissolution of the child's social group can hinder efforts at independence and autonomy. Being without peer support can send the child back to the nurturing qualities of the family nest. The child may regress for a brief period of time and depend on parents for both support and companionship. This may be the child's way of coping with new challenges, as well as adapting to a new environment.

If the fear of failure to make new friends becomes a reality, the child may react with feelings of shame and humiliation. The child may be left with an overwhelming sense of incompetence. These feelings may be concealed by defensive behavior or feigned boredom. Regardless of the manifested defensive or bored behavior, the perception of failure and incompetence can lead to lack of motivation to undertake new challenges. Even under the best of circumstances, being spurned by a friend or a friend-to-be is difficult for any human being. Practice and preparation cannot soothe the hurt of rejection.

A strong sense of self-worth, independence, and confidence can help change the crisis into a springboard for growth and development. For the majority of children, time will help them adjust to their new circumstances. Losses will be turned into gains and children will develop a new and satisfying network of friends and experiences.

Parents can help their child by discussing techniques for making new friends. Feelings of fear disguised by attitudes of standoffish-

ness or conceit can make an otherwise friendly child appear unap-
proachable. Smiles and friendliness, no matter how difficult under
the circumstances, can go a long way to attracting friends. An interest in learning about others and a willingness to meet new friends
half way can open a new world of camaraderie and companionship.
Parents should emphasize the harm of snap judgments about new acquaintances. Initial presumptions and conclusions can erode the opportunity to turn an acquaintance into a buddy.

Parents should keep in mind that no matter how big and emotionally strong the child may appear, he or she is still a child and
needs constant encouragement. Children need to be assured that they
will succeed. They must be reminded that they are loved and that
their parents understand how hard it is to make friends. Praise and
empathy are the keys to the parent/child communication process. A
secure, supportive, and understanding family relationship can help
relieve some of the tensions that the elementary school-age child
feels.

Books directed to middle childhood experiences can be helpful
resources. Separation from friends, fear of rejection, and making
new friends are common themes in children's literature. Middle
childhood is a time when children are learning to be true com-
municators. They use their newly acquired tools of reading and writing to exchange ideas and gain information. Books become a natural
means to a better understanding of the concept of friendship.
Changing a child's perception of a frustrating situation and promoting
cooperative, pro-social assertiveness may open opportunities for
learning and friendship.

It is important to keep in mind that each child is an individual
in his or her own right and therefore a variety of responses to another child are likely. Despite these individual differences, the previous paragraphs have highlighted commonalities shared among children. Healthy peer relationships are a primary part of middle childhood.

BIBLIOGRAPHY

Adcock, Don, and Marilyn Segal. *Making Friends*. Redmond, Washington: Exchange Press Books, 1986.

Makes practical suggestions on how to create an environment that encourages peer interactions and stimulates the development of children's social skills. Focus is on social development within a group setting. This book is available from the publisher at P.O. Box 2890, Redmond, Washington, 98073.

Ames, Louise Bates. *Your Seven Year Old*. New York: Delacorte Press, 1985.

Offers a general description of what parents can expect from their seven year old. It covers the child's relationships with others, especially siblings, peers, and parents. This book is one of a series covering the ages from one to seven. It is able to explicitly cover growth, health, nutrition, play, and school developments that take place during the seventh year. The author also offers answers to many of the typical questions asked by parents.

Asher, S., and J. Gottman. *The Development of Children's Friendships*. Cambridge, Mass.: Cambridge University Press, 1981.

Reviews relatively current research of peer relationships. Topics include children without friends, improving social skills, and the general impact of peers on child development. This is a well-written book for those with a serious interest in peer relationships.

Borba, Michele. *Self-Esteem: A Classroom Affair*. Vol. I. New York: Harper & Row, 1978.

Over one hundred ways to help children from the second grade down build self-confidence. All activities use low cost materials and have easy-to-follow directions. Helps children develop the skills necessary to get along with others and to feel good about themselves.

Borba, Michele. *Self-Esteem: A Classroom Affair*. Vol. II. *More Ways to Help Children Like Themselves*. New York: Winston, 1982.

Suggests ways to help children develop social skills such as making and keeping friends, handling disagreements, and working cooperatively. Designed to help children ages five to 10. Recommended for parents, teachers, and others who work with children.

Borman, Kathryn. *The Social Life of Children in a Changing Society*. Norwood, N.J.: Ablex, 1983.

The social life of children is viewed from a multidisciplinary perspective. This book presents an academic viewpoint. It is meant to be read by child development professionals.

Boys Town. *Helping Friendless Children*. Boys Town, Neb.: Father Flanagan Boys Home, 1980.

This booklet outlines how to teach basic social skills to socially isolated children. The presentation is simple and clear. Recommended for parents and teachers involved with the friendless child. Available at no charge by direct request from Boys Town.

Cartledge, Gwendolyn. *Teaching Social Skills to Children*. Elmsford, N.Y.: 1986.

Teachers who are encountering a lack of social skills in the children they teach will find this volume helpful. This book relates social skills training to children with specific problems.

Crary, Elizabeth. *Kids Can Cooperate*. St. Paul, Minn.: Toys'n Things Press, 1984.

Examines the skills necessary to teach children to resolve conflicts by themselves. Ways to motivate children to negotiate with each other are given. Written in a workbook format.

Damon, W. *The Social World of the Child*. San Francisco: Jossey-Bass, 1977.

Discusses the principal social relationships in a child's life. How these relationships govern the child's behavior is explored. Recommended for parents, teachers, and students of child development.

Dezin, N. *Childhood Socialization*. San Francisco: Jossey-Bass, 1978.

The dynamics of childhood socialization are reviewed in this volume. The author explores such topics as the importance of play and games during childhood and the genesis of the self. Interesting reading for anyone looking for information on this critical aspect of child development.

Dowrick, Peter. *Social Survival for Children*. New York: Brunner/Mazel, 1986.

Discusses the development of social skills and the consequences of poor social skills. Special chapters are devoted to the topics of the shy child, the fearful child, the aggressive child, and children interacting with adults.

Epstein, Joyce. *Friends in School*. Orlando: Academic Press, 1983.

Discusses the social processes of peer association, friendship selection, and peer influence. Though this volume deals mainly with the influence of peers in the secondary schools, much of the discussion can be applied to the later elementary school years. Students' personal characteristics and age are looked at in the context of friend selection and influence.

Field, Tiffany. *Friendships in Normal and Handicapped Children.* Norwood, N.J.: Ablex, 1984.

Based on a study that identified behaviors and qualities of young children that can enhance friendship-making skills. Chapters are written by leading researchers in the field of friendship development in children. A technical volume focusing on the young child.

Leahy, Robert. *The Child's Construction of Social Inequality.* Orlando: Academic Press, 1983.

Discusses topics such as understanding differences within friendship and inequalities in children's prosocial behavior. For educators and psychologists.

Neuman, Susan. *Exploring Feelings.* Atlanta: Humanics Limited, 1983.

A unique activity book that helps children explore their feelings about their friends, family, and themselves. Exploring feelings promotes a healthy self-image. For parents and teachers for use with young children.

Rubin, Kenneth H., and Hildy S. Ross. *Peer Relationships and Social Skills in Childhood.* New York: Springer Verlag, 1982.

Applies research to the common assumption that children's social skills grow and develop with age. Although the main concern is the emerging social relationships among siblings, children and children, and parents and children, the discussion is not solely limited to this area. The text is a point of departure for further study. For professional and interested persons.

Schaefer, Charles, and Howard Millman. *How to Help Children with Common Problems.* New York: Van Nostrand Reinhold, 1985.

Two well-known experts in child development tackle the everyday problems faced by children. Advice is given in a nontechnical, down-to-earth style. Peer relationships, sibling rivalry, and immature and insecure behaviors are but a few of the topics covered.

Schaffer, H. *The Child's Entry into a Social World.* Orlando: Academic Press, 1984.

Mutuality between children and their social partners is the theme of this volume. Discusses ways in which social interactions change through the course of development. This book provides an overview of the acquisition of social skills through the early years of childhood.

Scott, Sharon. *PPR--Peer Pressure Reversal: A Guide to Developing a Responsible Child*. Amherst, Mass.: Human Resource Development Press, 1985.

The author, former Director of the Dallas Youth Diversion Program, has developed a method to help children cope with peer pressure and remain on the right track. Focus is on teaching the skills necessary to avoid or reverse peer pressure and reinforcement of social skills.

Walker, Will. *The Walker Social Skills Curriculum: The Accepts Program*. Austin, Texas: Pro-Ed, 1983.

Designed for teaching classroom and peer social skills to handicapped and non-handicapped kindergarten through sixth grade students. Behavioral management procedures and direct instruction provide the format for this program. A 30 minute demonstration tape is available, explaining the program's application from start to finish.

Youniss, James. *Parents and Peers in Social Development*. Chicago: University of Chicago Press, 1980.

The perspective of Sullivan and Piaget provides theoretical guideposts for the professional researcher. The impact of peer relationships on personal and social development during the childhood years is studied.

Zimbardo, Philip, and Shirley Radl. *The Shy Child*. New York: Doubleday, 1982.

The authors give tips to prevent shyness as well as suggest a program of intervention for the shy child. Parents and teachers might find this book useful in bringing out and helping to actively integrate the shy child into a peer group.

SCHOOLING IN MIDDLE CHILDHOOD

What is the function of school? Most people would answer to provide an education; to teach children how to read and write and do
arithmetic. No doubt this answer is right since schools serve the
function of teaching cognitive skills. Ideally, they facilitate the
achievement of the child's intellectual potential. By the time children finish elementary school they have put in several thousands of
hours of classroom time. During these hours they have learned much
more than to read and write. They have learned general skills such
as obeying authority. They have come to share basic societal values
and norms.

From the first day of school children are told how to act; "sit
quietly, pay attention." As one child exclaimed "all you do all day
long is mind." The expectations of the adults in charge (teachers,
principals) suggest the manner of behavior that is acceptable in the
classroom and school. In other words, children are given a role to
play. This role includes learning social conventions. If they perform
their role properly, they validate the expectations of the institution
and are rewarded for it. They are labeled "good" child and "good"
student. If they ignore those expectations or act contrary to them,
they pay the penalty. The label becomes "bad" child and "bad" student.

It is through this system that schools communicate the values
and norms of society at large. These values supplement and generally
support the value system of the home.

In studying the development of children's social conventional
behavior, researcher and moral theorist, E. Turiel, has found children
perceive sequential levels in which they first accept then reject the
validity of conventions.[1] This research suggests that the early
elementary school child has a descriptive understanding of social conventions based upon observations of people in various situations.
They see regularities in daily behavior and think of these as compulsory. They have no understanding of the social significance of conventions. For example stealing candy from the grocery store and
wearing a dress are the wrong way for a boy to behave. By age
eight or nine there is a negation of social convention. The fact that
there is a social regularity no longer implies it is a compulsory regu-

---

[1]William Damon, *Social and Personality Development* (New York:
Norton, 1983), 288-291.

larity. Social conventions are thought to be arbitrary regulations of society. For example, the child realizes that most elementary school teachers are women, but also realizes that there is no compelling reason why this is so. The mandatory force of the previous level of social reasoning is gone; however, children at this age still do not understand the social significance of conventions. This understanding begins around 10 to 11 years of age, when children realize that conformity to rules is necessary to maintain social order. At this stage rules or conventions are thought to be maintained in order to maintain a coherent society. By around age 12 or early adolescence, this implicit acceptance again changes. Children begin to look at the validity or morality of rules. Breaking convention is not thought to be an important violation of social order, as long as one does not do something immoral. Conventional norms are arbitrary whereas moral norms are binding.

This sequential development process continues through the end of adolescence when the young adult comprehends that conventions can help people live harmoniously and that though specific rules or conventions are arbitrary, they are useful. Children at this point in time are able to relate their personal world to the societal realm.

Though the child may be the recipient of society's value system as reflected by the schools, he or she by no means plays a passive role. The child actively seeks out adult guidance and acceptance. As Barbara and Philip Newman state in their book, *Development through Life: A Psychosocial Approach*, "sometimes it is very difficult to know the "real" personality of a middle-school-age child because the child is so preoccupied with presenting what has just been learned to be socially desirable."[2]

How the child presents himself depends a great deal on the school environment. This includes the teacher/student interactions and expectations, the structure of the classroom, the teaching methods used, and the learning style of the student. On examining student/teacher interactions it is important to remember that the classroom is the child's immediate environment in the school. The teacher rules the classroom. How he or she (and in most cases elementary school teachers are shes) relates to each student sets the emotional climate of the classroom. Teachers communicate many classroom rules directly, many however are tacit. Elementary school-age children must be able to pick up these tacit rules and responses in order to succeed. Some children do this better than others. They may find fitting into the teacher's expectations easier than a child less adept at social skills and communicating.

The belief that teachers treat all children the same, unfortunately, is an educational myth. Teachers, even in their attempts at fairness, are human. They are influenced by children's personal

---

[2](Homewood, Ill.: Dorsey, 1984), p. 258.

characteristics, academic performances, and gender. Patricia Minuchin and Edna Shapiro in their review of school as a context for social development in Paul Mussen's *Handbook of Child Psychology*,[3] cite the following research findings:

> Teachers are generally attached to students who are achieving, conforming, and make few demands. They show concern for students who make demands appropriate to classroom activity, but are indifferent to invisible and silent children and have little interaction with them. They reject children who make many demands considered illegitimate or who tend to be "behavior problems."

Minuchin and Shapiro continue with

> Teachers expect certain kinds of behavior from high achievers and different behavior from low achievers.... High achievers are given more opportunities to participate in class and more time to respond. They receive more praise for giving the right answers and less criticism than low achievers. Low achievers are expected not to know and not to participate and are given less opportunity and encouragement for doing so.

The authors comment further

> That teachers treat boys and girls differently in school has been well documented.... Elementary school teachers interact more with boys than girls ... boys received both more instructional and controlling messages from teachers, who also expressed more negative involvement with the boys in their classes.... When children solicited attention the teacher responded to boys with instructions, giving girls fewer directions but more nurturance.

Teachers may be influenced by the personality and behavior of individual children, but they too are judged by children. Children spread the reputation of a teacher both to other children and the home. In general, teachers who are strict or unfair or are overly partial to certain students are judged negatively by elementary schoolers.

The elementary school setting also encourages student/student interaction.Hundreds of interpersonal exchanges take place in the school each day. The school is the major social institution and challenge for the child. For the majority of children, most interactions

---

[3] "The School as a Context for Social Development." (New York: Wiley, 1983), p. 226-228.

will be happy. Some, however, will inevitably cause unhappiness or embarrassment. Peer values persist and are a potential interference with learning. Much of what is learned in school is the product of student/teacher and student/student interactions. The quality of social context, and the social impact on learning, can be affected by the learning environment of the classroom, teacher attitudes, and characteristics of the particular children. Children in traditional learning environments are generally organized for competition whereas children in more flexible environments show more helping attitudes and behaviors. Elementary school children quickly pick up the social conventions of their classroom in particular, and the school in general.

The physical structure of the classroom reflects the policy of the school, philosophy of the teacher, and impacts the student. Research has indicated that children seated in windowless rooms feel more negative about school and aggressive toward it. Children who are seated down the middle and across the front of the classroom are directly in line with the teacher's pattern of interaction. These students will be more actively involved by the teacher. More flexible teachers allow more socialization in the classroom. When children are seated face-to-face, cooperation is facilitated. When too many children cluster into one area of the room, cooperation may turn to competition. Overly crowded conditions threaten a child's sense of personal space and can produce conflict and competition. To encourage an optimal learning experience for children, elementary school teachers must work to match their physical milieu, philosophy, and curriculum.

The way a teacher teaches affects the way a child learns. Learning style describes how children perceive information and in what way they are motivated. For many years educators held the belief that all children could be taught the same subject, at the same level, in the same manner. Current research has shown that this cookie-cutter approach may not fit the needs of most students.

Under the cookie-cutter system differences in approaches to learning are considered flaws to be corrected. In actuality there are no flaws but different basic ways of perceiving, processing, and transmitting information or subject matter. In understanding the child's learning style, the teacher shows respect for the child. As a child learns, self-confidence and self-esteem flourish. For example, in new situations some children logically think their way through step by step. Other children react and tend to "sense" their way through. Some people perceive information visually, aurally and/or kinesthetically. Nancy Reckinger[4] of California State University has studied

---

[4]Nancy Reckinger, *Parents' Record of Educational Progress; How to Insure Your Child's Success in School* (Fullerton: California State University, 1984), 33-35.

student approaches to learning. She has separated these approaches or styles into four basic categories. Reckinger estimates that approximately three quarters of all students are equally divided between practical learners and active learners. Practical learners prefer structure, routine, and step by step directions. This type of student does well with an organized teacher who generally assigns seats, gives direct, concrete experiences and specifically explains. The practical learner tends to be obedient, conscientious, and wants to please the teacher.

Active learners are spontaneous, and resourceful. They like the freedom to work in their own way. They dislike direct supervision and paper and pencil work. Achievement in subjects such as reading and writing can flourish if the subject matter is related to active projects. This type of student is more likely to ask a "How does this work?" type of question, rather than a "What, who and why?" question.

Reckinger estimates that the remaining one quarter are divided into the categories of personal style learners or focused style learners. The personal style learner focuses on people. This student tends to be sensitive, idealistic, understanding, and needs positive, warm feedback from the teacher. Discussion, role playing, and cooperation are preferred to competition. Too much criticism can cause physical illness in this student. Whereas personal learners are very concerned about how teachers perceive them, focused style learners are not greatly concerned about what their teachers think. Frequently this type of student is thought to be cold, and a loner. The focused style learner values intellectual abilities and needs to know and be competent. Often this student may choose to ignore subjects not perceived as important and, as an independent learner, sets own goals as to what should be learned. This student often prefers math, science and technology. Why and how questions are what interests the focused learner.

A child may have traits in one or more of these categories. However, most students will primarily identify with one category over the others. These categories and traits compose an individual child's learning style.

Research on brain hemisphere functioning suggests that brain hemisphere specialization can influence one's learning traits. Early research by the Nobel Prize winner Roger Sperry[5] suggested that the right and left halves of the brain process information differently, have different modes of thinking, and that people have right or left preference when initiating learning. Dr. Ronald Rubenzer writing for

---

[5]Raymond Corsini, ed., *Encyclopedia of Psychology*, 4 vols. (New York: Wiley, 1984), 3:357.

Gifted Children Monthly[6] suggests that people with left brain prefer-
ences will have different learning characteristics than those with
right brain preference. Though both hemispheres of the brain are
necessary for learning, remembering, and utilizing information, children tend to predominantly use the thinking mode of one side of the
brain over the other side. Traits associated with the left side include being verbal, logical, structured, analytical, motivated by external rewards, and task orientated. Traits associated with preference for the right hemisphere of the brain include being unstructured, artistic, visual, motivated by satisfaction, idea orientated, intuitive and imaginative. Rubenzer suggests that parents and teachers
can promote more creative thinking in children by asking speculative
questions. Beginning a question with "what if," "why not" and "how
many ways" will encourage the child to think. Who, what, why,
when, where and how only challenge the child's recall.

What an overwhelming task it would be for an elementary
school teacher during the first few months of school to decide which
children best fit a general category of learning style or preference!
Teachers discover this as they work individually with the student and
personally get to know each student. This process can be facilitated
by past school anecdotal records that comment on learning style, parent communications of their child's learning style needs, and the best
match of student learning style to teaching style.

The same way that students have individual ways of receiving
and processing the learning material, teachers have individual ways of
initiating and transmitting that material to their students. Reckinger's research[7] suggests the teaching style characteristics can go
hand-in-hand with learning style characteristics. In an article for
Journal of Children and Youth, she breaks down teaching style traits
into the categories of the practical teacher, active teacher, personal
teacher, and focused style teacher. Reckinger estimates that slightly
over half of all teachers use a practical style of teaching. Following
the role of the traditional school teacher, this individual is likely to
maintain authority, follow rules, establish a fixed routine, and favor
recitation drills and tests.

About one third of all teachers fall into the category of the
democratic, personal style teacher who builds self-esteem, stresses
learning by doing, individualizes instruction, and communicates caring
and enthusiasm. The active style teachers tend to be impulsive, value
competition, favor projects, contests, games, and are not concerned
with homework. Along with the active style, the focused style

---

[6]Ronald Rubenzer, "Left Meets Right In Whole Brain Thinking,"
Gifted Children Monthly, (August, 1985): 1-3.

[7]Nancy Reckinger, "Learning Styles For Parents And Teachers,"
Journal of Children and Youth, (Spring 1985): 21-26.

teachers comprise under 10% of the general teaching population. The focused style teacher uses lectures, tests, and a problem solving approach. He or she may be oblivious to the emotional climate of the classroom and use an impersonal approach to students. This type of a teacher can become impatient with the slow or boring student and a mentor to the bright student.

We cannot change a child's learning style or a teacher's teaching style. However, parents, students, and teachers can work together and accept and respect each others likes and differences. To force or coerce a child to change can damage their school success and feelings of self-worth. To gain understanding of how a child learns can maximize a child's school potential and self-confidence. A good match of teaching and learning style can convey to the elementary school child that the school can be a safe and exciting place to learn and that the adult authority is fair and trustworthy. As Donald Helms and Jeffrey Turner note in their book *Exploring Child Behavior*, "classroom harmony usually depends on the match between the values, temperaments and the personalities of the students and those of the teacher."[8]

No school is complete without its textbooks and reviewers of school textbooks have been critical of the way the world is printed on the text page. Frequent stereotyping of sex, race, and class, as well as idealistic portraits of a world without anger or moral questionings, result in a bland reading textbook. Children are not able to relate to, and therefore are not gaining maximum benefit from, the text. Educators and reviewers of textbooks, Saario, Jacklin and Tittle have stated in the Harvard Educational Review, "The real world is more varied than the one depicted in elementary readers.... Rather than limiting possibilities, elementary texts should seek to maximize individual development and self-esteem by displaying a wide range of models and activities."[9]

Boys' and girls' interest areas don't always mesh with the stories of the text. A good teacher can help to overcome these limitations by supplementing assignments to take in wider interest areas.

Along with texts in the classroom, come tests. Elementary school-age children are subjected to tests ranging from self-evaluation to standardized group testing. Are these tests accurate interpreters of comprehension and cognitive ability? Standardized group tests sample a wide variety of mental abilities such as verbal, mechanical, and numerical capabilities. The choice of which group test will be used lies with the administration of a particular school system. Parents who are interested in better understanding the stan-

---

[8](New York: Holt, Rinehart and Winston, 1981), p. 297.

[9]T. Saario, C. Jacklin and C. Tittle, "Sex-role Stereotyping In the Public Schools," *Harvard Educational Review* 43 (1973): 386-416.

dardized tests their children are given can go to their local library for a copy of Buros *Mental Measurement Yearbook*.[10] Buros provides a review of all major tests, identifying strong and weak points and the appropriate usage of each test. Parents should always look at their children's test scores in the context of the test given. Each test score should be accompanied by the component parts of the test scores. A child can score highly on many sub-tests and have the average test score brought down by scoring very low on one particular sub-test. A profile of how a child tested, as compared to other children the same age and grade, can give information as to the child's degree of success or failure.

For example, a third grade child might have an overall low score on a test taken by third through sixth graders. However, when compared to other third graders the score might compare favorably. John Glover in his book *A Parent's Guide to Intelligence Testing*[11] states "the value of test results increases as the amount of information imparted is increased."

School systems administer both achievement tests and intelligence tests. Parents should note the difference. Intelligence tests measure potential capacity to learn. Achievement tests measure what has been learned. Beyond standardized testing the elementary school child is exposed to hundreds of tests and quizzes on taught subject matter each year. Bright students without test anxiety might find these tests rewarding, reinforcing a positive self-image of doing well. Students with test anxiety, or who generally fare less successfully in school, can be negatively affected by poor test scores, reflected in poor grades. Poor grades alone are not a motivator for the child to work harder. In this context Benjamin Bloom in his book *Human Characteristics and School Learning*[12] writes that "the child approaches the next task in the series with marked reluctance. He expects the worst and is prepared for it. If it is painful enough, the task is avoided or approached with little enthusiasm and, if anything, marked dislike.... [The child] has little patience or perseverance when he encounters difficulties and takes little care and thoroughness in accomplishing the task."

Since grades impact on the child's feelings of competence and self-worth, teachers and parents should not only stress the final product of the "grade" but emphasize reaching personal goals of success. This means becoming process oriented as well as product oriented. Focus is on how much effort is put into the assignment and

---

[10]Oscar Buros, *Mental Measurements Yearbook* (Lincoln: University of Nebraska Press, 1986).

[11](Chicago: Nelson Hall, 1979), p. 24.

[12](New York: McGraw-Hill, 1976), p. 146.

how much the child has gained from the assignment. Over time a child who learns to enjoy the work will learn more and achieve academic improvement. Children who are working only for the grade aren't learning to enjoy learning.

Teachers who delineate what the student should be able to accomplish, under what conditions and to what extent, are more helpful to students than teachers who simply evaluate students in comparison to others in the class. The more definition and exactness the teacher uses in evaluation, the more able a student is in setting realistic goals for achievement.

Usually around the mid-elementary grades, homework is assigned. What does this accomplish? Parents and teachers alike generally feel homework helps to make the student more responsible and aids in the development of good work habits.

In general, the research on academic achievement and homework shows that homework does not harm; however, it might not do much good either. There appears to be no clear cut argument to support or negate the giving of homework to increase academic achievement during the elementary school years. Ideally, homework should be individualized for the needs of each student rather than all classmates taking home the same assignment and finishing it at different speeds with some learning from the assignment, others learning nothing at all.

Many teachers have found that individualized, independent projects allow students to select their own approach to a problem or topic. This approach generates excitement while allowing slower students not to fall behind and more advanced students to progress as fast as they are able.

Homework appears to have an added benefit not related to school but to the family. The *Harvard Education Letter* reported that an a Gallop Poll, 49% of parents said they regularly helped elementary aged children with homework. This is up from 1977, when only 37% claimed to offer a helping hand.[13] Parents who show positive support for their children's education have children more interested in education.

Academic underachievement or poor achievement can leave the child unready to proceed to the following grade level. Material that lays the groundwork has yet to be learned by the student. The question becomes is it beneficial or harmful for the elementary aged child to be held back to repeat a grade? Until the 1930s when concern for the psychological stigma of holding children back became accepted, retention was common. As many as half of all students enrolled in grades one through eight repeated a grade at least once in their academic careers. Current research shows no persuasive evidence that retention promotes learning. Studies on the psychological

---

[13]*Harvard Education Letter*, 1(1):1-3 (February, 1985).

impact of holding children back suggest that the retainee compared to other children has fewer friends and lower self-esteem.

Parents and school systems should encourage the academically lagging or emotionally troubled student to be given special help rather than repeating an academic year in the elementary school grades.

Delaying school entry and, to a lesser extent, the repetition of kindergarten can be beneficial. The youngest children in a class are at an academic disadvantage for the first eight years of schooling. The National Assessment of Educational Progress indicates that about 30% of those children who are in the youngest 1/12th of their class are held back, compared to 10% of those children who are in the oldest 1/12th of their class.[14] Late school entry allows the child time to mature. In general, more mature children function at a higher level. Giving the very young-for-grade child or the very immature child another year of nursery school or kindergarten can help to assure a successful elementary school experience.

Student pressure to do well and/or to do too much has led to a rapid rise in illness and stress in elementary school-age children. Psychological stress to achieve good grades and to succeed in numerous before and after-school activities ranging from sports to the study of music can leave children not having time to enjoy their childhood. Young children with chronic stress symptoms such as headaches and stomachaches are not uncommon. If school presents a consistent, unpleasant experience for the child, school phobia can develop.

Two types of school phobia appear during the elementary school years. The first is generally found in children during kindergarten or first grade. Its origins are thought to lie in a difficult parent/child separation. There may be anxiety and dependency on the part of both parent and child. The second develops from chronic difficulties at home or school. Symptoms of school phobia include persistent complaints of aches and pains around breakfast time that disappear shortly after school has begun and the child has remained home.

Children should not be allowed to develop a pattern of missing school. If symptoms persist, parents should review their child's activities to see what may be causing stress. If symptoms still do not subside parents should consider seeking outside help for their child starting with a visit to the child's teacher and the pediatrician.

Children need time to process all they have experienced. Time to think through their day; time to daydream. Parents should be cautious not to overschedule their children, but to allow them the freedom to pursue what interests them at their own pace.

Though children may spend their day in school, the presence of their family is felt throughout the elementary school experience.

---

[14]*Harvard Education Letter* 2(2):4 (March 1986).

Once children enter school they go from being the shining star in their family to one of many in the school group. The child learns new expectations and demands. These new experiences are reflected in behavior and attitudes at home. Suddenly, parents may find their words of wisdom usurped by what the teacher said at school. The teacher's remarks sound like gospel to the early elementary school child. This new attitude of independence can result in demands for added freedom and power at home. As the child gradually takes on new responsibilities there may be a new desire to cling to the old "blankey" or teddy bear for security. Parents should remember that as a child steps into the world of school and peers, they still remain their child's base to run to for emotional support and guidance.

The closer parents and teachers can bridge the gap between home and school, the easier the transition will be for the child. The easier it will also be to resolve any problems that appear along the path of the child's education.

Open communication amongst parents and teachers facilitate learning and problem resolution. Parents should not be hesitant to visit, call, or send a note to the teacher. Most teachers are very willing to involve parents in the classroom. Parents who are interested in knowing what is happening in the classroom can possibly volunteer an hour or two of time on a regular basis. If there are too many constraints on parents' time to volunteer services, they should find the time to meet with or call up the teacher before or after school. Parents should ask the teacher what he or she thinks of the child's school performance, give the teacher ideas as to what may be hindering the child's learning or what assignments and subjects excite and motivate the child. Parents may solicit from the teacher ideas as to what they can do to help their child, as well as give suggestions as to ways the teacher may be able to work with their child. Teachers and parents should follow through on whatever plan of action is decided upon.

Teachers are responsible for the learning experience of a classroom of children. They have limited time and resources. It is helpful if parents keep this in mind during parent/teacher discussions. It may be helpful for parents and teachers to involve the principal in discussions or a plan of action. Overseeing the learning experience and social environment of the school is part of the principal's job.

Occasionally a child may have a conflict with the teacher that is not easily resolved. Schools, for the most part, assume that students will adapt to a particular teaching style. If a child experiences failure, judgment is usually made about the child, not the teacher's teaching style or competence. Not every student and every teacher are compatible in teaching and learning styles. If the problem is severe it is probably better to move the child to another classroom where the child's learning and social life can proceed uninterrupted. This is a problem that requires the guidance and actions of the principal.

Parents should always remember that they know their child better than anyone else, and that they and their child have rights. Parents should not be intimidated by the school system. Children receive the most benefits when parents with high, yet realistic expectations work together with the school and their child. The parent-teacher relationship should not be adversary but complimentary. Prior to parent-teacher communications, it is wise for the parent and the teacher to ask themselves "If I were in their position, how would I feel, what would I want, and how could I achieve my objectives?" Mutual respect and honest interest are keys to facilitating communications.

Adults can enhance the school experience in the middle years by exercising faith and trust in children. Teachers and administrators must remember that schools have a strong impact on behavior at all developmental stages. As children learn to relate to teachers and other children and to regulate their behavior to the acceptable standards and rules and to cognitively conquer the tasks of academics, they are continuously changing and evaluating their own sense of identity, worthiness, confidence, justice, and morality.

Understanding and empathy for the child's point of view can help make school a more pleasurable experience and a place where all children can experience success.

BIBLIOGRAPHY

Adams, Paul, Judith Milner, and Nancy Schrept. *Fatherless Children*. New York: Wiley, 1984.

Provides a look at the causes of fatherlessness, such as divorce, death, desertion and unwed motherhood. The authors examine topics including school adjustment of the fatherless child.

Aiken, Lewis. *Psychological Testing and Assessment*. Rockleigh, N.J.: Longwood, 1985.

An authoritative sourcebook for those involved or interested in school testing. Reviews of over 400 tests are included. Theories of intelligence and personality, key individuals, and landmarks in testing are discussed. This book contains three separate indexes for easy referencing (test title, test topic, test author).

Alvino, James. *Parents' Guide to Raising a Gifted Child: Recognizing and Developing Your Child's Potential*. Boston: Little-Brown, 1984.

Though written for parents, teachers will find this excellent guide a helpful aid to working with the gifted child in the classroom. Advice on fostering creativity, and educational, challenging games suitable for the classroom are given. An extensive reading list is included.

Anatasi, Anne. *Psychological Testing*. New York: Macmillan, 1982.

The author outlines major principles of test construction, social and ethical implications of test use, and available types of testing instruments. Further areas of interest in this book include guidelines for test selection and outlines for test evaluation. Suggested reading for professionals working in psychological testing.

Aspy, David. *This Is School: Don't Feel--Don't Think--Don't Talk-- Line Up--Don't Get Involved*. Amherst, Mass.: Human Resource Development Press, 1986.

Offers a view of future education based upon a look at the past. Over 200,000 hours of classroom instruction over a period of more than 20 years were used as the basis for author's analysis. This book is geared to professional educators.

Aspy, David, and Flora Roebuck. *Kids Don't Learn from People They Don't Like*. Amherst, Mass.: Human Resource Development Press, 1985.

Surveys the teaching skills of several hundred teachers and the learning achievement of several thousand students. It attempts to target the main component of successful teaching. Professional educators will find this book most interesting.

Baron, Bruce. *What Did You Learn in School Today?* New York: Warner, 1983.

   What Did You Learn in School Today? helps parents answer that frequently asked question. This is a book that aids parents in guiding their children through the American educational system. It addresses detecting and analyzing learning problems and ways of correcting these problems. Published as a large-format paperback.

Beeman, Phillips. *School Stress and Anxiety.* New York: Human Sciences Press, 1978.

   Links theoretical views and empirical finding on school stress. School situations causing stress are examined. Stress-reducing intervention programs are discussed. Diverse topics such as the differential impact of stress, school stress, and minority children are discussed.

Bettelheim, Bruno, and Karen Zelan. *On Learning to Read: The Child's Fascination with Meaning.* New York: Knopf, 1982.

   The authors suggest that the American education establishment is responsible for the reading failures of many a young child. At the core of the problem is the system's failure to grasp the true uses of reading. This book is a stimulus for change. It provides provocative reading for parents and teachers.

Bissex, Glenda. *Gnys at Wrk: A Child Learns to Write and Read.* Cambridge: Harvard University Press, 1980.

   Details the development of learning to write and read from ages five to ten. The intertwining of writing ability and reading development are emphasized. Examples of the development of abilities in the author's child personalize the theoretical concepts. Bissex's observations are of interest to parents and educators.

Bloom, Gaston. *Stress in Childhood.* New York: Teachers College Press, 1986.

   Stress has become a frequent impairment to academic success for many children. Teachers are in a position to help children deal with the stress of today's lifestyles. This book provides an intervention model and many suggestions that teachers can use to alleviate stress in the classroom. Examples and case studies are given.

Bloom, Benjamin. *Developing Talent in Young People.* New York: Ballantine, 1985.

   Studies the question, "Are geniuses made or born?" Dr. Bloom, an internationally renowned educational researcher suggests that talent is greatly conditioned by environment, parents, and teachers. This makes interesting reading for parents and teachers.

Brown, Mac, and Carl Brown. *Reading Activities: From Teacher to Parent to Child.* Atlanta: Humanics, 1982.

Contains activities to help establish a home/school partnership for teaching children basic reading skills. Activities focus on visual and auditory discrimination, learning letter sounds, and phonics.

Caletta, Anthony. *Working Together; A Guide to Parent Involvement.* Atlanta: Humanics, 1976.

Working Together promotes a sense of trust between home and school. It stresses clear communications and reciprocity of relationships. Supplements to parent involvement programs such as child development guides and check lists are included.

Carlson, Mary. *Help! For Parents of Gifted and Talented Children.* New York: Good Apple, 1984.

Provides activities to help elementary school age children further develop their thinking skills. Activities can be used with all children, not limited to the gifted and talented. Parents and teachers might find this book helpful.

Christman-Rothlein, Liz, and Jane Caballero. *Back to Basics in Reading Made Fun.* Atlanta: Humanics, 1980.

Back to Basics offers an innovative approach to teaching beginning reading skills. There are over one hundred games and projects suggested to refresh reading curricula. Ideas given help to motivate early elementary students learning to read. This book is written for teachers.

Church, Ellen. *Learning Things.* Belmont, Calif.: Fearon, 1983.

Games that making learning fun are suggested for early elementary school children. Activities promote learning in language, math, and reading by developing perception and cognitive abilities. Introduction to each game or activity lists skill areas to be cultivated. This book is available in paperback.

Cohen, Dorothy. *The Learning Child.* New York: Vintage Books, 1972.

A guide to how children learn during the elementary school years. It incorporates the findings of major educational theorists and psychologists, with the author's experiences. Dr. Cohen is on the faculty of New York's Bank Street College of Education.

Comer, James P. *School Power*. New York: The Free Press, 1980.

An examination of the public school system and recommendations for intervention with techniques developed in two pilot programs in New Haven, Connecticut. Emphasis is on leadership training for principals, creative teaching techniques, and the need to stop blaming the students for failure.

Corsini, Raymond. *Encyclopedia of Psychology*. New York: Wiley, 1985.

This is a four volume reference source. Included is comprehensive coverage of educational psychology and testing. Over two thousand articles make this a major reference source in psychology.

Ehly, Stewart. *Peer Tutoring for Individualized Instruction*. Austin, Texas: Pro-ed, 1980.

Provides teachers with practical advice on establishing peer tutoring programs. How-to techniques, pointers on matching tutor to student, and program evaluation are discussed. Also included is a chapter on peer tutoring for special needs children.

Freeman, John. *The Psychology of Gifted Children*. New York: Wiley, 1985.

Explores theoretical and practical issues relating to gifted children and their education. Focus is on identifying the gifted, as well as the socio-emotional and behavioral development of these children. This book is interesting reading for professionals working with gifted children.

Gallagher, James. *Teaching the Gifted*. Rockleigh, N.J.: Longwood, 1985.

A guide to teaching gifted children by one of the most respected leaders in the field. Covers identification procedures, instructional methods, and materials. Also included are topics such as helping female students overcome math and science anxiety. Case studies are woven through the book.

Griffore, Robert. *Child Development: An Educational Perspective*. Springfield, Ill.: Thomas, 1981.

The focus of this volume is the relationship between concepts of child development and the process of education. Emphasis is on personality and cognitive development. This book is directed to teachers.

Gruber, Ellen. *Could I Speak to You about This Man, Piaget, a Second?* Atlanta: Humanics, 1979.

This practical book helps to clarify the ideas and theories of the late and renowned Swiss psychologist Jean Piaget. A helpful introduction to often difficult to understand theories. For students, teachers and parents.

Hegerman, Kathryn. *Gifted Children in the Regular Classroom: The Complete Guide for Teachers and Administrators.* New York: Trillium Press, 1980.

The author has written an activity manual for teachers working with gifted children in the regular classroom. Identification of gifted children is discussed. Suggestions for providing stimulating and appropriate learning experiences are given.

Hills, John. *Measurement and Evaluation in the Classroom.* Columbus: Merrill, 1981.

Provides guidance in the construction, use, and interpretation of classroom tests. This book has been designed with teachers in mind. A succinct, straightforward presentation, including topics such as accountability and the legal aspects of testing, makes this volume a useful reference.

Holt, John. *How Children Fail.* New York: Delta, 1982.

Holt perceives the classroom as "the scene of a continual battle in which teacher and child struggle to gain the advantage." Holt presents an alternative to bring the classroom back to a place for learning. John Holt's books were classics in the 1960's and are still interesting, thought-provoking reading.

Holt, John. *How Children Learn.* New York: Dell, 1986.

In the revised edition of this classic book, Holt explains how children make sense out of their world and how their learning process operates. This paperback book is interesting reading for parents and teachers alike.

Holt, John. *Teach Your Own.* New York: Dell, 1986.

This book is for parents who are interested in the alternative of home schooling. Step-by-step the author guides parents in taking children out of the school system, keeping them out, and teaching them at home.

Hoover, Kenneth H., and Paul M. Hollingsworth. *A Handbook for Elementary School Teachers.* Boston: Allyn and Bacon, 1982.

Teacher strategies flexible enough to fit into a variety of classroom settings are detailed in this easy to use handbook. Suggestions are given for teaching multiethnic children, encouraging parent involvement, and mainstreaming.

Horowitz, Frances, and Marion O'Brien. *The Gifted and Talented, Developmental Perspectives*. Washington, D.C.: American Psychological Association, 1985.

Describes the different approaches to educating gifted children. These include the alternatives of enriched curricula and accelerating the student through the standard curriculum. This book also addresses many of the problems of educating gifted children, such as lack of financing and unqualified teachers.

Kahn, Jack. *Unwillingly to School*. New York: Pergamon, 1981.

Presents an account of the failure of school attendance due to emotional causes. The perspective is from the viewpoints of psychiatry, social work, and education. Helpful for any professional dealing with school phobia or school refusal.

Kolvin, J. *Help Starts Here*. New York: Tavistock, 1981.

Techniques for the detection of the maladjusted child in the ordinary school setting are described. A method for the assessment of the results of treatment, as well as evaluation of treatment approaches are discussed. This is a technical book for the professional in psychology and education.

Languis, Marlin, Tobie Sanders, and Steven Tipps. *Brain and Learning: Directions in Early Childhood Education*. Washington, D.C.: National Association for the Education of Young Children, 1980.

Supports the use of a hands-on curriculum to accommodate children's different learning styles. Strategies are discussed to assist teachers in preparing activities which promote integration and active use of the right and left hemispheres of the brain.

Larrick, Nancy. *Children's Reading Begins at Home--How Parents Can Help Their Young Children*. Winston-Salem, N.C.: 1980.

Daily routines can be turned into educational experiences that encourage children to read. The relationship of reading to play is explored. Description of how reading is taught and the development of oral language skills are given. This is a helpful book for parents.

McGinnis, Ellen. *Skillstreaming the Elementary School Child*. Champaign, Ill.: Research Press, 1985.

Examines the social skill needs of children who display aggression, immaturity, social withdrawal, and other developmental lags in the classroom. The book advocates a method of structured learning for these children. Fifty specific social skills are addressed in the areas of dealing with feelings, friendship-making alternatives to aggression, and classroom survival. Recommended for teachers and other school personnel.

Mack, Faite R.P., and Melvin Wesley Wells. *Learning Games: Through Games-Objective Based*. Novato, Calif.: Academic Therapy Publications, 1981.

Discusses the combination of play and education. Over 200 lesson plans are included. Each contains step-by-step procedures, materials needed, and behavioral objectives. A good book for teachers.

Maffei, Anthony. *Classroom Computers*. New York: Human Sciences Press, 1986.

This practical, illustrated guide shows how computers can be used in the classroom to make teaching more effective and learning more efficient. Reasons for integrating computers into the classroom are clearly presented. The fundamental tools used in classroom computer teaching and lesson plans dealing with specific subject matter application are discussed.

Martin, Robert J. *Teaching through Encouragement: Techniques to Help Students Learn*. Englewood Cliffs, N.J.: Prentice-Hall, 1980.

Effective teacher-child interaction is the focus of this book. Practical suggestions are given for coping with non-productive student behavior. Hints are given on encouraging communications and responsibility. Useful to teachers and parents.

Montessori, Maria. *The Secret of Childhood*. New York: Ballantine, 1982.

Maria Montessori describes the child and discusses the materials and techniques required to release learning potential. This is a warm and sensitive book reflecting the brilliance of the author. Truly a classic.

Moore, Raymond. *Home Grown Kids*. New York: Good Apple, 1984.

A practical guide to teaching children at home. Advice is given on interweaving everyday resources and experiences into the home schooling curriculum. For people interested in the home-schooling movement.

Mosse, Hilde L. *The Complete Handbook of Children's Reading Disorders: A Critical Evaluation of Their Clinical, Educational and Social Dimensions*. New York: Human Sciences Press, 1982.

A helpful resource for anyone involved with a child experiencing a reading disorder. In two volumes the reading process is examined. Specific disorders and syndromes frequently associated with organically based reading problems are reviewed, as well as unspecific and general symptoms frequently associated with reading, writing and arithmetic disorders.

National Education Association. *National Education Association's Yellow Book*. New York: Garland, 1984.

A descriptive account of educational software that has been tested by the NEA and found to be technically reliable and to perform all advertised functions, instructionally sound, and presented in an interesting manner. Each program listing includes systems requirements, contents, and price. A helpful, handy guide.

Newmark, Charles. *Major Psychological Assessment Instruments*. Rockleigh, N.J.: Longwood, 1985.

Up-to-date information is given on the 10 most widely used intelligence and psychological tests. Includes tests such as the Kaufman Assessment Battery for Children and the WISC-R. Comparisons are made of the various tests. Background on standardization, validity and reliability are included.

Ollila, Lloyd O. *The Kindergarten Child and Reading*. Newark, Del.: International Reading Association, 1977.

Should reading be taught at the kindergarten level? This book raises the issues surrounding this controversial question. *The Kindergarten Child and Reading* is of interest to parents, teachers and administrators.

Papert, Seymour. *Mindstorms: Children, Computers and Powerful Ideas*. New York: Basic Books, 1980.

Two major themes run through this work. One states that children can master the use of computers. The other suggests that computers can change the way children learn. A timely book.

Peterson, Penelope. *Social Context of Instruction*. Orlando: Academic Press, 1983.

Centers around the themes of the organization of instructional groups and the processes of instructional groups. The authors consider such issues as the characteristics of students in forming the groups, the size of instructional groups and the mechanisms through which instructional groups have their effects. For educators and psychologists.

Pickering, C. Thomas. *Helping Children Learn to Read: A Primer for Adults*. New York: Chesford, 1977.

Answers for parents the question of how children learn to read. Sample pages from textbooks illustrate the process used in schools. Ideas are given for coordinating home and school activities.

Powell, Marjorie. *Teacher Attitudes*. New York: Garland, 1986.

Traces the development of teachers' attitudes toward themselves and their students for the past decade and a half. There are over 1500 citations. There is an introduction that provides an overview discussion of the topic. Teacher characteristics, effects of teacher attitudes, and influences on teacher attitudes are among the many topics covered.

Powell, Marjorie, and Joseph Beard. *Teacher Effectiveness*. New York: Garland, 1985.

A comprehensive listing of literature on teacher effectiveness from 1965 through 1980. There are over 3000 listings. Topics included within the area of teacher effectiveness are teacher expectations, effective classroom management, teacher behavior, student-teacher interaction, and teacher impact on student achievement and attitudes.

Rubin, Judith. *Child Art Therapy: Understanding and Helping Children Grow through Art*. New York: Van Nostrand Reinhold, 1984.

Analyses how children use art to communicate their feelings. The author demonstrates how children can have a better understanding and liking of themselves through art therapy. Though targeted for art therapists, this book may prove insightful to the classroom teacher.

Rutherford, Robert B., Jr., and Eugene Edgar. *Teachers and Parents: A Guide to Interaction and Cooperation*. Boston: Allyn and Bacon, 1979.

The premise of this book is that effective teacher-parent interaction involves cooperation and exchange of information in order to promote trust and resolve conflicts. The authors provide an approach to problem solving and open communications.

Samuels, Shirley. *Disturbed Exceptional Children*. New York: Human Sciences Press, 1981.

A comprehensive guide to the emotional needs and problems of exceptional children. Teachers are helped to recognize children's psychological problems and develop individualized remediation programs.

Sanoff, Henry. *Learning Environments for Children*. Atlanta: Humanics, 1981.

This book explains how to create a pleasant, efficient, stress-free learning environment. Guidelines are given that are flexible and adaptable to differing educational needs.

Sarafino, Edward. *The Fears of Childhood, A Guide to Recognizing and Reducing Fearful States in Children*. New York: Human Sciences Press, 1986.

Describes what children fear, why fears develop, and ideas for intervention. Teachers and parents can learn how to help children overcome their anxieties and phobias and be better able to cope. A straightforward and practical book.

Sattler, Jerome. *Assessment of Children's Intelligence and Special Abilities*. Rockleigh, N.J.: Longwood, 1981.

Sattler offers information on 71 of the major individual intelligence and special ability tests for children, such as the McCarthy, WISC-R, and Stanford-Binet. Chapters are also devoted to testing and ethnic minorities, the retarded, the gifted, brain-damaged, and psychologically troubled.

Schiavone, James. *Help Your Child Read Better*. Chicago: Nelson-Hall, 1977.

Written for parents who want to increase their child's reading proficiency. This is an easy-to-use guidebook filled with games and helpful hints. Basic facts about how children learn to read are explained.

Schultz, Edward, and Charles Heuchert. *Child Stress and the School Experience*. New York: Human Sciences Press, 1983.

Describes the stress that frequently accompanies a child's experience with the educational system. The authors propose an intervention program that warrants attention. A well-thought-out study of the difficulties in children's lives and how they influence school success.

Stuart, Irving, and Lawrence Abt. *Children of Separation and Divorce: Management and Treatment*. New York: Van Nostrand Reinhold, 1981.

Though the general context of this book is to provide comprehensive analysis pertaining to the legal, social, and emotional consequences of marital breakups, it has been included in this section for its discussion of the school's role in helping children cope with divorce. This book is suggested for educational personnel.

Velten, Emmett, and Charlene Sampson. *Rx for Learning Disability*. Chicago: Nelson-Hall, 1978.

A down-to-earth guide for parents and teachers. This book defines commonly used jargon, simplifies theories, and gives workable suggestions on how to deal with common learning disabilities.

Weinberg, Richard, and Lynn Weinberg. *Parent Prerogatives: How to Handle Teacher Misbehavior and Other School Disorders*. Chicago: Nelson-Hall, 1979.

A manual for parents encountering intimidation, hostility, or incompetency in the schools. The authors demonstrate how to handle these problems and tell what rights parents can demand. A book that breaks through the jargon to the practical.

Williams, Doris. *Handbook for Involving Parents in Education*. Atlanta: Humanics, 1985.

A guidebook for those concerned with the role parents play in their children's education. Topics include the parent as a model educator, and parents as volunteers. Presented from an historical perspective to the latest trend.

Wilson, Gary. *Parents and Teachers: Humanistic Educational Techniques to Facilitate Communication between Parents and Staff of Educational Programs*. Atlanta: Humanics, 1974.

Consists of a series of structured experiences which can be used separately or as a total program promoting parent involvement and increased parent/staff interaction. A good springboard for developing effective cooperation.

Wolman, Benjamin. *Handbook of Intelligence*. New York: Wiley, 1985.

Looks at the area of intelligence research from its beginnings to the present. Investigative reports on topics include the validity of intelligence tests, minority children and intelligence testing, group testing, and the educational application of intelligence tests. This is a high level compendium geared to the researcher or educator familiar with the area.

SOCIETAL IMPACT ON MIDDLE CHILDHOOD

It is not easy to raise a child--or to be a child--in today's "high-tech" world. Family structure and values have changed. Sexual and moral standards seem to be constantly declining. There is great concern over the environment, the economy, and the threat of nuclear annihilation. There is an ever-increasing emphasis on technical sophistication. Too many children are being encouraged to grow up too soon too fast.

Such changes in society cannot help but have an effect upon our children. Some of these effects are beneficial while others have a negative impact on middle childhood. The changing structure of the family is unquestionably of major significance. It is therefore addressed as a separate chapter on *Family Interactions*.

A number of Child Development experts have expressed grave concerns that these technological advances and societal attitudes are changing middle childhood from a period of calm, steady development to one of stress. Children in the middle childhood years are especially vulnerable to society's values. These are the years when children are increasingly exposed to school and community, influenced by peers, and are developing a sense of competence and self-identity.

Eda LeShan, an authority on child guidance and education, writes in *The Conspiracy against Childhood*[1] that

> In our demands for ever accelerated learning at an ever earlier age, we are robbing children of their birthright, eliminating several stages of childhood, so vital to health and growth. We are forcing premature adulthood on young people, stuffing them with precocious knowledge at the expense of developing into whole human beings with sensible moral values.... We live in an era in which science and technology represent a new religion, a road to salvation.... Technology has made possible a world of over-abundance and affluence that has changed the world for our children.

As technology becomes increasingly sophisticated, parents are being encouraged to teach their children skills before they are physi-

---

[1]Eda J. LeShan, *The Conspiracy against Childhood*. (New York: Atheneum, 1967), 1-34.

ologically and developmentally appropriate, schools are emphasizing test taking, and children are increasingly pressured to achieve early or be regarded as failures.

Parents may unwittingly encourage their children to unrealistic achievement as a means of compensating for their own failure, perceived or actual. Whatever the motivation, this increased pressure on children too often results in stress-related illness, drug and alcohol abuse, and even suicide.

Children need time to just enjoy being children. Sports, scouting, music lessons, and other organized activities are an important part of growing up. Children in the middle years need group activities with their peers, and outlets for their emerging skills. What they don't need is a schedule limited to highly structured, adult-organized activities. Adults tend to stress competition while peers are more apt to emphasize compromise. The philosopher Rousseau is thus quoted in *The Conspiracy against Childhood*[2]

> Hold childhood in reverence and do not be in any hurry to judge it for good or ill. Give nature time to work before you interfere with her method. Nature wants children to be children before they are men. If we deliberately depart from this order we shall get premature fruits which are neither ripe nor well flavored and which soon decay. We shall have youthful sages and grown-up men. Childhood has ways of seeing, thinking, and feeling peculiar to itself; nothing can be more foolish than to substitute our ways for them.

Television is a prime example of technology that has profoundly affected the lives of children, both positively and negatively. Television can promote social growth and thinking skills; it can be used to enhance and motivate reading; foster visual literacy; and television can teach children to discern visual details and to orient themselves in space.

Much has been written about the harmful effects of television on children. Reading ability can be hindered if children watch TV to the exclusion of reading. In fact, research cited by Palumbo[3] suggests a negative correlation between heavy television viewing and learning. A child's social development can be hindered if TV is used as a babysitter. The excesses of violence on television can lead to aggressive behavior and can cause children to become insensitive to brutality. Constant bombardment by commercials can give children

---

[2]Ibid., p. 326.

[3]F.M. Palumbo, *Television: Effects on the Development of Children*. Children Are Different: Behavioral Development Monograph Series: Number 14. (Columbus, Ohio: Ross Laboratories, 1985), p. 3.

"the gimmies," thus encouraging inappropriate purchases. Eventually, children become suspicious, if not cynical, of advertising and its profit motive. Television can promote other undesirable behaviors, such as the use of tobacco, alcohol, drugs, and promiscuous sex. Negative stereotypes of minorities, women, and the aged, along with the glorification of undesirable role models can present a skewed view of American life. Since most television programming is geared to the 18-49 age group, much of what young children are exposed to is beyond their capability to evaluate and comprehend. The noted child psychologist David Elkind[4] is concerned that

Television gives children entree into experiences they never would have had without it.... But exposure is one thing and understanding is another.... Making experiences more accessible does not make them more comprehensible.

Indeed, television can be blamed for many of the problems of today's children. This should not, however, negate the value of television as a potent learning tool. Television is well-suited to the developmental capacities of school age children because it stimulates both visual and auditory learning.

The skills and qualities that can be developed by television must be balanced by other means of communications and other less passive activities. All dimensions of a child's developmental level must be considered. The following advice is offered by Greenfield[5] to parents

Because television is so powerful as a learning tool, it is all the more important that children be exposed to high-quality programming that (1) does not go beyond their emotional maturity, and (2) provides fantasy or fact that will be useful, not detrimental, to life beyond the television set.... Parents can do much to improve the effects of television by being selective about what shows children watch and by discussing programs to encourage children to watch critically and thoughtfully.

As with television, video games and computers are examples of technology with both negative and positive ramifications. Video

---

[4]David Elkind, *The Hurried Child: Growing Up Too Fast Too Soon.* (Reading, MA: Addison-Wesley, 1982), p. 77.

[5]Patricia Marks Greenfield, *Mind and Media: The Effects of Television, Video Games and Computers.* The Developing Child Series, Jerome Bruner, Michael Cole & Barbara Lloyd, eds., (Cambridge: Harvard University Press, 1984), p. 94.

games and video arcades have been chastised as being wasteful, expensive, and unwholesome. They can also be characterized as dynamic, creative, and challenging. While opponents describe the games as "shoot-'em-ups" and the arcades as "dens of iniquity," advocates stress that the games develop sensorimotor skills and that the arcades are social gathering places.

Video games for home usage do not generate as much criticism as the arcade variety. Games that are played on television sets are often enjoyed by other family members as well, thus promoting family interaction. A major criticism of video games for the home computer, however, is that their cost limits their accessibility.

The attraction of video games, according to Greenfield[6] is (1) the appeal of their visual action; (2) the interactive nature; (3) the child's sense of "active control"; and (4) most importantly, the presence of a goal.

Computers, like video games, are attractive to children because they are dynamic and interactive. In addition, they can be programmed. Educational uses include learning softwear, word processing, and programming. Computer literacy can enhance cognitive learning and prepare children for the adult job market.

Most schools now routinely utilize television as a teaching aid and introduce computer literacy at the elementary school level. This has necessitated major endeavors in teacher training and massive financial outlays. Parents who are unfamiliar with computers may feel inadequate.

Movies and records are other examples of controversial media. It is believed that television, more than films, hastens inappropriate and premature behavior. This is because children tend to identify with the role in television, whereas in movies, they identify with the actor portraying the role. Music on records is directed primarily at the unconscious or subliminal level of children's awareness. The melody as well as the lyrics provide an "escape" from stress, boredom, and/or emotional loneliness.

The changes in sexual and moral values in society affect not only adolescents, but preadolescents as well. Children are becoming sexually active early; the number of pregnancies in girls under age 14 is increasing. There are numerous and complex reasons why these changes have occurred. It is easy to blame television and the media for glorifying sexuality; advertising undoubtedly does glamourize sexual attractiveness and sensual encounters. Even preadolescents are exposed to enormous pressures to be sexually active.

Another issue to consider is the fact that, largely due to improved nutrition, physical (and sexual) maturation is occurring earlier than in the past. Concurrently, our high-tech lifestyle tends to reduce both the quantity and quality of adult interaction with children

---

[6]Ibid., p. 108.

at a time when children need and want guidance from their parents in order to understand these physical changes and their feelings about sexuality.

Children from nine to twelve years of age may appear quite sophisticated sexually. In fact, parents may be fooled into thinking that their children this age must already have adequate information about sex and sexuality--which is rarely the case. Children this age are eager for such information, but they often are reluctant to ask for it.

Changing sexual and moral standards have added to the controversy over sex education. Everyone agrees that sex education is needed; the controversy centers over *who* should impart the information and *how* it should be imparted. Primary responsibility for teaching about sexuality and morality is ultimately with the parents. There is a tendency today to deal with a problem by teaching about it at school. The schools have an important role in imparting correct information, but ideally this should be in addition to, not in place of parental guidance. Parents should be made aware that children learn about sexuality and morality throughout childhood from them, both directly and indirectly. Children's attitudes are shaped more by the atmosphere of the home and the behavior of the parents than by conversations with them.

Society's double standard on sexuality is especially confusing to preadolescents, who developmentally feel so intensely about moral issues. Parents often present different moral messages to their daughters than to their sons. They may demand abstinence from their daughters while encouraging sexual experience for their sons. Most parents today neither expect nor wish their 10-12-year-old children to be sexually active. Yet, these same parents permit--even encourage--early dating and the wearing of clothing and other trappings, often seductive, intended for adults. Children are confused by these mixed messages regarding expected "grown up" behavior.

How much influence do parents of today actually have in shaping the behavior of their school-age children? Are parental standards always undermined by peer pressure? This is not a simple issue. Once again, it is essential to examine the effects of changing family lifestyles on the quantity and quality of parent-child interaction. Today, fathers commute farther and travel more in their jobs, and more mothers work outside the home. Between 1960 and 1987, the percentage of women in the work force rose to 55.8 percent from 35.7 percent, according to the Bureau of Census and Labor Statistics. World War II seems to have marked the start of society's "acceptance" of women, especially mothers, working outside the home. Today, well over half of the women in today's work force have young children.

No two families are alike in how they view this issue or how they deal with it. Even the child development experts do not agree. Rita Kramer, in her book entitled, *In Defense of the Family: Raising*

Children in America Today,[7] makes the general statement that parents are not helpless before social, political, and cultural forces which seem beyond their control; they need not be overwhelmed by them. On the other hand, Kenneth Keniston, writing for the Carnegie Council on Children in *All Our Children: The American Family Under Pressure*,[8] maintains that it is not parents who are responsible for their family life or their children's fates. He views children as the victims of society and its pressures.

As for peer pressure, Sharon Scott[9] points out that the three characteristics of children most likely to be affected by negative peer pressure are: (1) Boredom, (2) Alienation from family, and (3) Low self-esteem. Scott cautions, however, that not all peer pressures are destructive. In fact, most peer pressure relationships are positive and beneficial. Peers often act as a voice of conscience in decision making. The need for peer relationships can vary among children.

Another aspect of society that affects middle childhood is increased violence against children. Child abuse occurs within the family, while sexual abuse of children can occur within or outside of the family. These abuses cross all social, racial, economic and cultural lines. Situational stresses on the family unit often contribute to child abuse situations, while deep-seated emotional disorders often underlie sexual abuse. Regardless of the cause(s), it is now necessary to provide children with safety education that, in a sense, teaches children not to trust adults. Additional self-protection safety instructions are necessary for the growing number of "latchkey children" who are home alone (or in charge of younger siblings) for extended periods of time while parents work.

Current societal attitudes and practices affect school-age children in differing ways, depending on family economics. In the last decade, more women have married later and postponed parenthood until they have completed their education and established their careers. The children of these more affluent, better educated women are now of school age, and are often the recipients of extravagant expenditures for clothing and amenities. They are often expected to be "gourmet children," as perfect in output as in input. Too often, this search for perfection results in undue pressure and competitiveness.

At the other end of the economic spectrum, there are many families forced by divorce, desertion, or single parenthood by choice,

---

[7](New York: Basic Books, 1983), p. 4.

[8](New York: Harcort Brace Jovanovich, 1977).

[9]Sharon Scott, *PPR: Peer Pressure Reversal*, (Amhurst, Mass.: Human Resources Development Press, 1985), p.6.

to subsist on welfare and under substandard living conditions. These children often lack the emotional support and intellectual stimulation to reach their potential in life. There are growing numbers of families with children among the homeless or living in welfare hotels.

Yet another characteristic of our present society is increased mobility. Whether a (child's) change in residence is the result of parental promotion or unemployment, it will still have a profound effect on a child of this age. According to Alvin Toffler in *Future Shock*,[10] it is not unusual for a family to move every three or four years. This lack of "putting down roots" can impart a lack of commitment to a child. There is a tendency in mobile families to form limited relationships with people and limited involvement with community endeavors. A related phenomenon that threatens the development of a sense of security in children is the emergence of a "throw-away society"; the rapid rise and use of disposable products is seen as another example of accelerated change. Toffler defines "Future Shock" as "what happens when the familiar psychological cues that help an individual to function in society are suddenly withdrawn and replaced by new ones that are strange or incomprehensible."

There is no doubt that the years of middle childhood are affected by the changes occurring in society. We do not live in a static society. But change is not necessarily harmful; it may be difficult to accept, but it is often the impetus to growth.

An examination of societal effects on middle childhood is bound to highlight those effects that are harmful, and hence, more noticeable. It is important to keep in mind the many advantages that school-age children have today, particularly opportunities for learning as a result of improved technologies.

In reality, America is still not the child-centered nation it claims to be. However, children in this society *are* a major concern. Children's rights and child welfare are, and will continue to be, major issues, for children are society's greatest hope.

---

[10]Alvin Toffler, *Future Shock*. (New York: Random House, 1970), p. 12.

120 Resources for Middle Childhood

BIBLIOGRAPHY

Barcus, F. Earle. *Images of Life on Children's Television: Sex Roles, Minorities and Families.* New York: Praeger, 1983.

Examines the extent to which television reflects the traditional and changing patterns of family life. This study is sponsored by ACT (Action for Children's Television). A summary of the research literature relevant to each topic is included, as well as a substantial bibliography.

Blume, Judy. *Letters to Judy: What Your Kids Wish They Could Tell You.* New York: G.P. Putnam's Sons, 1986.

A collection of letters from children confiding their concerns about friendships, families, health, sexuality, and other problems. The author is a writer of books that are popular with children and young adults. The letters were written to her in response to real-life situations described in these books.

Colao, Flora, and Tamar Hosansky. *Your Child Should Know: Protect Your Children From Assault and Crime.* New York: Berkley, 1986.

Suggests ways to teach children strategies for safety, such as how to recognize suspicious behavior, and how to defend themselves.

Edelman, Marian Wright. *Families in Peril: An Agenda for Social Change.* Cambridge: Harvard University Press, 1987.

Describes the overall and comparative status of black and white children and families in America today. The author is president of the Children's Defense Fund, an advocacy group aimed primarily at protecting the rights of poor children. This book is comprised of the W.E.B. DuBois Lectures of 1986, sponsored by the Ford Foundation. It destroys commonly held myths about broken homes and poor families, and proposes changes in government policies.

Elkind, David. *The Hurried Child: Growing Up Too Fast Too Soon.* Reading, Mass.: Addison-Wesley, 1982.

Explores the special stresses on children of the eighties, how and why these stresses evolved, and how to identify and help these children. This eminent child psychologist warns parents that, "Children need time to grow, to learn, and to develop." A disturbing book, yet essential reading for anyone concerned about children.

Gerzon, Mark. *A Childhood for Every Child: The Politics of Parenthood.* New York: Oederbridge and Lazard, 1970.

Describes how modern society interferes with all stages of a child's development. Gerzon believes that in today's technology, children are not allowed to grow "naturally," resulting in a repressive dehumanization of growth. States that today's "technical parent" is only partially accountable for his child's growth; that he delegates authority--and blame--to other specialists, such as doctors, teachers, and even the food industry. This book is an indictment *against* technology and *for* children. This is a most unusual book, and is fascinating reading. The author was a radical in the 1960's, and is now concerned about priorities of parenthood, and the future of children in our technological society.

Grollman, Earl A. *Latchkey Children*. Boston: Beacon Press, 1986.

Highlights the growing problem of unsupervised children--the complex causes, the safety and psychosocial problems, and offers advice to remedy the problem.

Hechinger, Grace. *How to Raise a Street-Smart Child: The Parents Complete Guide to Safety on the Street and at Home*. New York: Fawcet Crest, 1984.

Offers reassurance, tips, and practical advice to parents for coping with theft, mugging, sexual abuse, traffic problems, school bullies, child molesters, and television violence. This book is based on interviews with police, school safety personnel, neighborhood safety groups, and parents of victims. Recommends sensitive ways to protect children without frightening them.

Kuczen, Barbara. *Childhood Stress: Don't Let Your Child Be a Victim*. New York: Delacorte Press, 1982.

Stresses management techniques for children that are designed and adapted for parents to use in helping their children develop stress defenses. The premise of this book is that children in today's society are bombarded by stress-provoking situations--more to learn, more to worry about, more choices, temptations, and pressures from families and peers. References are included for each chapter.

Litwin, Susan. *The Postponed Generation: Why American Youth Are Growing Up Later*. New York: William Morrow, 1986.

Analyzes the social, economic, and emotional factors in our culture that rewards ambition and individualism. The author characterizes modern youth, raised in affluence, a sense of entitlement, and postponed responsibility, as a "floundering generation."

May, Rollo. *Love and Will*. New York: Norton, 1969.

The author is concerned that apathy is replacing love, and that advances in technology are undermining a sense of will.

Mead, Margaret. *Culture and Commitment: A Study of the Generation Gap.* Garden City, NY: Doubleday, 1970.

Asserts that the electronic media, with its capability to rapidly and freely transmit information, is replacing the older generation as a source of information for the young. A provocative book by this noted cultural anthropologist, warning that the natural curiosity of children is being replaced by cynicism or even arrogance.

Opie, Peter, and Iona Opie. *Children's Games in Streets and Playgrounds.* London: Oxford University Press, 1969.

Examines the negative results on middle childhood when play time is as completely organized and supervised as study time. The authors express concern for children who grow up in a society where they are no longer needed for vital chores, and where they are consumers rather than producers. Questions the priorities of parents and society on position and possessions rather than qualities of character.

Packard, Vance. *Our Endangered Children: Growing Up in a Changing World.* Boston: Little Brown, 1983.

Warns parents that our society is not adequately preparing children for adulthood. Examines the radical social changes that affect our attitudes, our institutions, and the structure of our homes.

Postman, Neil. *The Disappearance of Childhood.* New York: Delacorte, 1982.

Criticizes the mass media, and its influence on aggression and sexuality on children. The author, a professor of Media Ecology at New York University, writes a critical and thought-provoking account of the subtle ways in which contemporary society, especially the media, is threatening our children. Postman states that a media blitz prevents parents from safeguarding children from adult secrets of aggression and sexuality. He urges parents to stand firm against the bombardment of media influence on their children's dress, behavior, language, attitudes, physical appearance, and desires.

Rimm, Sylvia B. *Underachievement Syndrome: Causes and Cures.* Watertown, Wisc.: Apple, 1986.

Blames parental overindulgence, overprotection, and permissiveness for this syndrome characterized by lack of confidence and disorganization. Provides case study vignettes of parents who extend their own aspirations onto their children, thus unwittingly conferring upon them extensive power to manipulate their adult world before they have the knowledge, wisdom, and maturity to wield such power.

Spock, Benjamin. *Raising Children in a Difficult Time: A Philosophy of Parental Leadership and High Ideals*. New York: Norton, 1974.

Urges parents to maintain their ideals of discipline, creativity, imagination, friendliness, lovingness, and the joy of giving, as well as mutual respect and open communication with their children. More of this famous pediatrician's "common-sense" approach to the problems caused by rapidly changing customs, such as sexual behavior, drug use, and family structure.

Winn, Marie. *Children without Childhood*. New York: Pantheon, 1983.

Examines the shrinking boundaries between childhood and adulthood, the decline in respect for parental and adult authority, the early loss of children's innocence, and the increasingly early involvement of children with the dangers of adulthood. This is a disturbing book about unchildlike children and their newly unprotected position in today's changing society.

Youngs, Bettie B. *Stress in Children: How To Recognize, Avoid and Overcome It*. New York: Arbor House, 1985.

Characterizes stress as a disease of the twentieth century. Author provides numerous charts, tables, and self-administered quizzes that spotlight how to recognize stress and overcome it. This book includes numerous exercises for the child alone, or for parent and child together on problem solving skills, time management, proper nutrition to prevent stress, and exercise to reduce stress. There is a grade-by-grade list of "School Stress Signals" from kindergarten through high school.

AUTHOR INDEX

Abt, Lawrence, 110
Ackerman, Nathan W., 56
Adams, Paul, 101
Adcock, Don, 69, 84
Aiken, Lewis, 101
Akins, Dianna, 11
Alvino, James, 101
Ames, Louise Bates, 29, 84
Anatasi, Anne, 101
Anderson, Peggy, 11
Anderson, Valerie, 69
Asher, S., 84
Aspy, David, 101
Attebury, Jean, 69
Axline, Virginia, 69

Bahr, H.M., 57
Baker, Bruce, 69
Balter, Lawrence, 11, 51
Banks, Jean L., 54-55
Barcus, F. Earle, 120
Baron, Bruce, 102
Beard, Joseph, 109
Beckwith, Glenwood J., 69
Beeman, Phillips, 102
Behrstock, Barry, 11
Bellows, Richard S., 59
Bereiter, Carl, 69
Berg, Barbara, 56
Berman, Claire, 56
Bernard, Harold W., 29
Bettleheim, Bruno, 25-26, 28, 56, 70, 102
Bindler, Ruth, 11
Bissex, Glenda, 102
Bloom, Benjamin, 96, 102
Bloom, Gaston, 102
Bloom-Fishbach, Jonathen, 56
Bloom-Fishbach, Sally, 56
Blume, Judy, 120

Boden, Margaret, 38
Bond, Tim, 70
Borba, Michele, 84
Borman, Kathryn, 84
Bornstein, Berta, 28
Boston Children's Medical Center, 11
Bottomly, Jim, 70
Boys Town, 85
Brace, Edward, 12
Brazelton, T. Berry, 57
Brody, Jane, 12
Bronfenbrenner, Urie, 49, 70
Brooks-Gunn, Jeanne, 12
Brown, Carl, 103
Brown, Catherine Caldwell, 70
Brown, Mac, 103
Brunner, Jerome, 68
Buros, Oscar, 96

Caballero, Jane, 70, 103
Calderone, Mary, 12
Caletta, Anthony, 103
Call, Justin D., 31
Capaldi, Frederick, 57
Caplan, Frank, 63
Caplan, Theresa, 63
Caplow, Theodore, 57
Carlson, Mary, 103
Cartledge, Gwendolyn, 85
Chadwick, B.A., 57
Chess, Stella, 28, 37, 40, 42
Christman-Rothlein, Liz, 103
Church, Ellen, 103
Clark-Stewart, Alison, 28, 42, 68
Coffin, Lewis, 12
Cohen, Dorothy H., 28, 37-38, 42, 103
Colao, Flora, 120
Collins, Glenn, 53-54

TITLE INDEX